Thanks for Talking Dirty with the Queen of Clean®

For orders other than by individual consumers, Pocket Books grants a discount on the purchase of **10 or more** copies of single titles for special markets or premium use. For further details, please write to the Vice President of Special Markets, Pocket Books, 1230 Avenue of the Americas, 9th Floor, New York, NY 10020-1586.

For information on how individual consumers can place orders, please write to Mail Order Department, Simon & Schuster, Inc., 100 Front Street, Riverside, NJ 08075.

Talking Dirty
with the
Queen of Clean®

LINDA COBB

POCKET BOOKS
New York London Toronto Sydney Singapore

The author gratefully acknowledges and thanks the mothers and grandmothers who have passed many of these recipes down from generation to generation. These and other recipes have been collected and organized into this book. Thanks for *Talking Dirty with the Queen of Clean.*

The sale of this book without its cover is unauthorized. If you purchased this book without a cover, you should be aware that it was reported to the publisher as "unsold and destroyed." Neither the author nor the publisher has received payment for the sale of this "stripped book."

 POCKET BOOKS, a division of Simon & Schuster, Inc.
1230 Avenue of the Americas, New York, NY 10020

Copyright © 1998 by Linda Cobb

Published by arrangement with The Win Holden Company

All rights reserved, including the right to reproduce this book or portions thereof in any form whatsoever. For information address The Win Holden Company, 6836 South 38th Place, Phoenix, AZ 85040.

ISBN: 0-7434-1830-1

First Pocket Books trade paperback printing September 2000

20 19 18 17 16

Queen of Clean® is the registered trademark of Linda Cobb and is the property of Queen and King Enterprises, Inc.

POCKET and colophon are registered trademarks of Simon & Schuster, Inc.

Cover photo by John Hall
Cover design by Carolyn Lechter

Interior illustrations by Jeff Jones

Book designed by Helene Berinsky

Printed in the U.S.A.

My grateful thanks to:

My husband John, The King. You put the magic in my life and the joy in my heart. You can talk dirty to me anytime!

My Mom, The Queen Mother and my best friend. Thanks for the *gift of gab,* your laughter and your gentle, loving heart.

My Dad (1905–1995). You taught me to live my life as a person, not as a girl, and you were way ahead of your time. I owe you so much, Dad. You will be in my heart forever.

My cousin Charlene. What can you say about a woman who changed your diapers when you were a baby and still loves you!

David and Janette; Victoria; Pat, Laura, John and Justin; Nancy and Drew; Nanette, David and Patrick. These children and grandchildren are the gifts that we share with each other every day. They are the reason we smile, the reason we cry, and the reason we rejoice. God bless them!

Win and Carolyn Holden. "Only those who can see the invisible, can do the impossible." You saw the invisible in me and made all things possible. Your friendship is one of our greatest gifts.

Alan Centofante. You came, you saw, you believed and you convinced others. Thank you.

My KTVK-TV, *Good Morning Arizona* family. You created a monster—thanks guys!

My mentor, Gloria Pitzer, whose help and encouragement started me on this great adventure.

L. Michael Moretz, my former business partner and friend, who introduced me to real dirt and taught me all he knew about cleaning and disaster restoration.

Zack, The Palace Pussycat/Research Assistant. Without his tireless efforts the chapter on pet stains and problems could not have been written. Thanks, I think . . .

Judith Curr, President and Publisher, Pocket Books; your vision for "Talking Dirty" exceeded our dreams. I just love it when people have character and talent beyond my expectations, and that's exactly what our experience with Judith and Pocket Books has been.

Brenda Copeland, started out as my editor at Pocket Books, a stranger, but was really a friend in waiting. Her ability, warmth and sense of humor made this a totally wonderful, first-class experience.

All of our friends who understood why we couldn't come out and play.

And, to all of you who have Talked Dirty with The Queen of Clean®.

Because of all of you, it is good to be Queen!

— Linda Cobb

Contents

Contents

Foreword

My mother always used to say, "Don't play in the mud!" I think if she had known the Queen of Clean, she wouldn't have stressed so much.

Linda Cobb reminds me of those two brothers in the film *City Slickers* . . . you know, the ice-cream kings. "Give us a meal," they'd say. "We'll match it with the perfect ice cream flavor. Salmon? No problem: vanilla bean. Beef tenderloin? That's easy: cherry walnut."

The Queen does the same with stains! "Rust on clothes? A no-brainer! Lemon juice and sunshine. Musty books that smell? Come on, challenge me! Clay cat litter."

This woman can get the stink and the stain out of anything. The Queen even makes laundry attractive. It's hard not to love someone who finds so much joy in filth.

Parents, get ready to let your kids make mud their friend! I'm just glad Linda Cobb is mine.

—TARA HITCHCOCK, *Good Morning Arizona,*
KTVK-TV 3, Phoenix

More Foreword

The third Thursday of every month is a special day on our little morning radio show. That's when the Queen of Clean invites our listeners to "talk dirty to her."

She is one of the most popular guests we've ever had. After all, have you ever met someone who uses things like Tang™, lemon juice and Massengill™ to clean? Neither have we. And that's why we love our favorite Ol' Dirt Bag, Linda Cobb.

All hail the Queen of Clean!

—BETH McDONALD AND BILL AUSTIN,
Beth and Bill in the Morning,
KEZ 99.9 FM Radio, Phoenix

Please Note: I hope these tips provide the answer to many of your household problems. However, total success cannot be guaranteed in every case. Care and caution should be exercised when using chemicals, products, and formulas presented in this book. All cleaning treatments should be tested prior to application, in an inconspicuous place. This is highly recommended and strongly encouraged. Please read and follow all information contained on product labels with care. Linda Cobb, The Win Holden Company, and Pocket Books hereby disclaim any liability and damages from the use and/or misuse of any product, formula, or application presented in this book.

Talking Dirty
with the
Queen of Clean®

1

Beating the Bathroom Blues

Over the years I have found that there is one room that generates question after question and that room is the bathroom.

Once, when I was eating in a wonderful little Chinese restaurant, the proprietor—an elderly Chinese gentleman—followed me into the ladies' room to see if I thought his bathrooms were clean. He was using the methods that I had recommended on television and was making his own cleanser from my recipe. Let me tell you, his bathrooms were spotless! It made me think that of all the rooms in your house, the bathroom is probably the room that most guests always see and have the most private time to observe. I have tried virtually every cleaning product on the market and developed many of my own "Queen's concoctions"—what follows are the best and easiest cleaning tips I can offer.

Cleaning Fiberglas™ Showers and Tubs

Heat white vinegar until it is hot, but not too hot to pour into a spray bottle and work with. Spray it on the shower and tub heavily. Wait 10-15 minutes and then moisten a scrubbing-type sponge with more of the vinegar and scrub down the shower, using additional heated vinegar as necessary. Rinse well and dry.

Removing Hard-Water Marks

Many plastic-type tubs have a dimpled slip-proof bottom that defies cleaning. I have found that using a good gel cleaner or a mild cleanser, such as the homemade types listed on page 14, and a piece of fine drywall sandpaper (looks like window screen) works the best. Cut the sandpaper into a workable size, apply the cleaner and rub. Use this only on dimples in plastic and Fiberglas™ tub and shower bottoms.

Stubborn Spot Remover for Showers

For stubborn shower spots and scum buildup, use a dry soap-filled steel wool pad on a dry shower. Do not allow water to become involved in this process, as it will cause the steel wool pad to scratch. Follow up with the vinegar process described at the beginning of this chapter.

Keeping Plastic Showers Clean

To make shower upkeep simple, apply a coat of car wax. Do not use this on the floor of the tub or shower. After showering, use a squeegee to wipe down the shower door and walls, and your shower will stay clean and you'll have fewer problems with mildew.

Cleaning Porcelain Tubs

To clean and polish a porcelain tub and remove stains, make a paste of powdered alum (available in drugstores) and water. Rub well, as if using cleanser. For stains, make a paste of powdered alum and lemon juice; apply and let dry, then moisten with more lemon juice and rub well. Rinse thoroughly.

Borax and water is also a great cleaner for porcelain. Make a paste and rub well, then rinse.

Keeping Tile and Grout Clean

You can keep ahead of grout cleaning if you use a dry typewriter eraser on dry grout to remove mildew and stains as they appear. For bigger problems, make a paste of baking soda and chlorine bleach and apply to the grout. Let dry and then rinse. Do this in a well-ventilated area, using care near carpet or fabric. Even the fumes of chlorine bleach can remove color from towels left hanging in the tub area.

Tile and Grout Cleaner

Combine 2 parts baking soda, 1 part borax and 1 part hot water, adding additional water as necessary to form a thick paste. Apply to the tile and grout and scrub with a soft brush. Rinse well.

Cleaning Soap Scum and Mildew Off of Plastic Shower Curtains

Put the shower curtain in the washing machine with one cup of white vinegar, ¼ to ½ cup of your favorite liquid laundry detergent, and several old, light-colored towels. Fill the washer with warm water and run through complete wash and rinse cycle. Remove from the washer and hang on the shower rod immediately.

Cleaning Mineral Deposits from the Shower Head

Fill a plastic sandwich bag with undiluted white vinegar. Tie this around the shower head and leave overnight. In the morning remove the bag, scrub the head with a brush and it's ready to use.

Cleaning Chrome Faucets

Use white vinegar on a cloth or sponge to remove water spots and soap scum. Dry and buff with a soft cloth. Rubbing alcohol is also a great spot remover. Apply, then dry and buff.

To shine chrome or any metal fixture in a hurry, use a used dryer fabric softener sheet on a dry fixture.

QUICK TIP..
Put ½ cup of baking soda down the bathroom drain and follow with the vinegar in the plastic bag—great drain opener! Wait 30 minutes then flush with water.

Removing Hair Spray Residue

You can use this formula to remove hair spray residue from any hard surface—vanities, tile, floors, walls, etc. Mix a solution of ⅓ liquid fabric softener and ⅔ water in a spray bottle. Spray on the surface to be cleaned, and wipe. Not only does it remove hair spray, it also acts as a dust repellent and shines vanities beautifully!

Removing Bathtub Decals

Lay a sheet of aluminum foil over the decals and heat with a blow-dryer on high. Work up the edge of the decal with a dull straight-edge (credit cards work great) and keep applying the heat as you pull. If the decal is stubborn, lay down the foil as necessary and heat well and peel again. To remove the residue try petroleum jelly, denatured alcohol or nail polish remover. Test these products in a small area first before applying.

Cleaning Shower Door Tracks

Plug the drain holes in the door track with a little bit of paper towel made into a ball. Pour in undiluted white vinegar. Let this soak for 30 minutes, unplug the holes and rinse the track with a spray bottle of water and run a rag down it. This will flush the accumulated build-up out of the track.

Toilet Tips

If you have indoor plumbing, then you have to clean the toilet once in a while, whether you like it or not. Follow these tips and it will be a breeze:

Tang™ Tune-Up

To keep your toilet clean and your dog happy, put several tablespoons of Tang™ Breakfast Drink in the toilet before you leave for work or at bedtime. Let it soak, use your toilet brush to swish around under the rim, and flush. The great thing about this is you don't have to worry if the kids get into the toilet bowl cleaner.

Removing Hard-Water Rings

Shut off the water at the toilet tank and flush. Spray undiluted white vinegar around the inside of the toilet, then sprinkle borax onto the vinegar. Let soak about 30 minutes and then scrub with a piece of fine drywall sandpaper (looks like window screen—available at hardware stores and home centers). If you have an old hard-water ring you may need to repeat this several times.

Plop-Plop-Fizz-Fizz Cleaning

Drop a couple of denture-cleaning tablets into the toilet and let sit overnight. Brush under the rim with your bowl brush and flush.

2

Kitchen Duty

I don't think there is a room in the house that gets messy faster than the kitchen. So let's clean up!

Appliance Magic

Many of us have white appliances in the kitchen. In order to keep them from yellowing, try this formula when you clean the exterior.

Combine:

      8 cups of water
      ½ cup of chlorine bleach
      ½ cup baking soda
      2 tablespoons borax

Wash white appliances thoroughly (using care around carpet or fabric), rinse well and dry.

• Rubbing alcohol makes a great cleaner for the exterior of all types of appliances. Use care around flames.

• Club soda is a wonderful polish for the exterior of appliances. It doesn't have to be fresh and have fizz; even if it has lost its carbonation it works great.

• Don't grab your everyday dishcloth to wipe down appliances; it will transfer grease and smear the finish.

Cutting Boards

Remove odors from breadboards by wetting and then rubbing with a little dry mustard. Let sit for a few minutes and then rinse. To disinfect breadboards, especially wood, keep a spray bottle with 1 quart water and 3 teaspoons of liquid chlorine bleach. Spray on, let sit at least 5 minutes, and then rinse with hot water.

Broiler Pan

For quick, easy, neat cleaning, put the broiler pan in a plastic garbage bag and lay some paper towels on it. Spray with ammonia, close bag and leave overnight. In the morning, open bag (away from face, remember the fumes), wipe with the towels that are in the bag, remove, wash broiler pan and throw out the rest of the mess.

Burned-On Casseroles

Fill the casserole or pan with hot water and throw in several used dryer fabric softener sheets. Let soak (even overnight), rinse and wash.

Automatic Coffeemakers

Depending on how often you use your coffee pot and how hard your water is, you may want to do this once a month to once every 3 months.

Fill the water reservoir with undiluted white vinegar. Place a filter in the coffee basket and turn the pot on. Allow about half of the vinegar to run through and then shut off the pot. Let it sit for about 30 minutes, then turn the coffemaker on and allow the balance of the vinegar to run through. Clean the pot out well, fill the reservoir with fresh, cold water and allow it to run through. Run the fresh water through twice.

To Clean the Glass Pot

Use lemon and salt and rub with a sponge, or use baking soda and lemon juice or water and rub with a sponge. Rinse well.

To Clean the Basket and Other Parts

For white plastic units, soak any removable parts in hot water with dishwashing liquid and about ¼ cup of chlorine bleach. Soak about 30 minutes and rinse well. This helps remove the staining and oils. For dark-colored coffeemakers, use dishwashing liquid and about ¼ cup of white vinegar in the same manner as above.

Chrome Burner Rings and Guards

Remove the burner rings from the stove. Lay a single sheet of paper toweling on each pan and moisten with ammonia. Place them in a plastic bag and close the bag. Leave for several hours or overnight. Open bag (pointed away from face, please) and remove the parts. Wash, rinse and dry.

Dishwashers

To remove that milky film from glassware and clean the inside of your dishwasher, follow this procedure:

Fill the dishwasher with your glassware (no metal, please). Use no dishwasher detergent. Put a bowl in the bottom of the dishwasher and pour in 1 cup of household bleach. Run through the wash cycle, but do not dry. Fill the bowl again with 1 cup white vinegar and let the dishwasher go through the entire cycle. Now you have the film removed from your dishes and the dishwasher clean in one easy step.

Dishwasher Odor

Sprinkle borax in the bottom of the dishwasher and leave it overnight. Using a damp sponge, use the borax to wipe down the inside of the dishwasher, door and gaskets. No need to rinse, just do the next load of dishes.

Dishwasher Rust

To remove rust from the inside of the dishwasher, fill both detergent cups with Tang™ Breakfast Drink and run through the normal cycle. If rust is bad, several treatments may be required. When doing this don't put dishes or detergent in the dishwasher.

Dishwasher Spot Stopper

To keep your dishes spot-free, use this formula. Combine the following ingredients in a container with a lid:

    1 cup borax
    ½ cup baking soda

To use: Add 1 teaspoon of the mixture to the dishwasher along with your regular dishwasher detergent.

The Pain of Drains

This is the best nontoxic drain opener you will ever use. Pour 1 cup of salt (table salt, rock salt, any kind) and 1 cup of baking soda down the drain. Follow with a kettle of boiling water. If the problem is congealed grease, it will be gone immediately. For the very best results don't use the drain for several hours. If you need a stronger product, use 2 tablespoons of washing soda (available where laundry products are sold) dissolved in 1 quart of hot water and pour it slowly down the drain. Flush with hot water after 10 minutes.

Once-a-Month Drain Cleaner

Once a month, pour a handful of baking soda into the drain and add ½ cup of white vinegar. A small volcano will erupt. Cover the drain for several minutes and then flush with cold water after 30 minutes.

Cleaning the Disposal

Keep your garbage disposer clean and free-flowing by filling the sink with 3 inches of warm water and mixing in 1 cup of baking soda. Drain it with the disposal running.

Using the Plunger the Easy Way

Yes, there really is a special way to use a plunger to make it work more effectively. Close the overflow to the sink (usually in the front of the sink) by plugging it with an old rag. If you don't do this, the water will go down one hole and come back up the overflow. Fill the sink with 4-5 inches of water. Put the cup of the plunger over the drain and press down hard. Then pull the handle up, push down again and repeat 10 to 12 times. Adding a little petroleum jelly around the rim of the plunger gives even better suction.

Microwave Magic

To clean your microwave quickly and simply, wet a dish-cloth and place it in the center of your microwave. Turn on high and allow the cloth to sort of cook for about 30-40 seconds. The steam that this creates will help loosen any hardened spills and you can then use the heated cloth to wipe the inside clean. A note of caution: Don't try to use the cloth immediately; it will be very hot. This is a great way to disinfect your dishcloth, too.

Deodorizing the Microwave

To give your microwave a clean, fresh smell, place a bowl of water in it and add 3 or 4 slices of fresh lemon or 2 tablespoons of lemon juice. Cook on high for 30-60 seconds.

For the very worst odors, such as burned popcorn, place vanilla extract in a bowl and microwave for at least 30 seconds. Leave the door closed for 12 hours, remove the vanilla and wipe down the inside of the microwave.

The Smoking Oven

When something runs over in the oven and starts smoking and smelling, grab the salt. Sprinkle on a heavy layer of salt and continue cooking. The smoke and odor will stop immediately. When done cooking, close the oven and wait overnight. The next day you will be able to lift out the spill with a pancake turner!

Cleaning the Oven

Preheat oven to 200 degrees and leave on for 15 minutes. Shut off and leave door closed. Fill a shallow glass dish with ammonia and place on the top shelf. On the lower shelf place a pan filled with 2 cups of boiling water. Close the oven door and leave the pans inside 2 hours or overnight. Remove ammonia and water; make a paste of ammonia, ½ cup baking soda and 1 cup white vinegar. Spread paste over surfaces and leave on for about 15 minutes. Scrub with a sponge and steel wool pad (if necessary), then rinse. This even works on heavily soiled ovens.

Making Your Own Cleanser

For a great non-abrasive scouring powder for disinfecting, combine:

> 4 parts baking soda
> 1 part borax

Store in a shaker container.

For a nontoxic grease-cutting scouring powder, combine:

> 4 parts baking soda
> 1 part washing soda

Store in a shaker container.

Cleaning and Protecting Cooktops

I receive so many questions about cleaning cooktops that I decided to devote a section just to that. Actually, glass and smooth-top ceramic surfaces are fairly easy to clean if you follow a few rules when dealing with them.

Clean the surface only when it is cool, with either dishwashing liquid, a paste of baking soda and water (3 parts baking soda to 2 parts water) or a specially formulated cooktop cleaner. Apply this with a paper towel or soft cloth.

Rinse thoroughly and towel dry. Do not use a soiled dishcloth or sponge to wipe the top; it may leave a film, which can cause discoloration the next time it is heated. If this discoloration occurs, remove it with a specially formulated cooktop cleaner.

Burned-on soil can be removed with a razor-blade scraper. Avoid abrasive cleaners and pads.

If your cooktop is in really bad shape, you will have to take more drastic action before you can have cleaning ease.

You can try a product called Bon Ami®, which comes in a can, much like cleanser. This product can safely be used on mirrors, windows, windshields, etc. It has a mild pumice action. Use it very carefully with a soft, wet rag to remove heavy soiling. You can also use a mild ammonia solution along with a scrubbing-type sponge. Another product that will help remove stains and burned-on food is non-gel toothpaste, applied with a soft cloth.

Follow up these cleaning procedures by washing with dishwashing liquid and water and rinsing well. Rinsing with club soda will put a nice shine on the top surface.

I have found a wonderful product called Invisible Shield® Surface Treatment. Using this allows you to do what I call "preventive cleaning." You apply this, and in the future when you clean, spills and burned-on food bead up. It makes your stovetop surface react as if it were nonstick cookware—spills wipe off with nothing more than a damp cloth. You can safely use this on all surfaces except wood and paint—even glass! Call 800-528-3149 to find out where it is sold in your area.

QUICK TIP ....

To remove stains from nonstick cookware, boil 2 tablespoons of baking soda, ½ cup of white vinegar and 1 cup of water for 10-15 minutes. Re-season the pan with salad oil.

Refrigerator Odors and Spills

When you wipe out the refrigerator, always use a cloth or sponge moistened with white vinegar. It leaves a clean, fresh scent and helps prevent mildew.

A dab of vanilla, lemon or orange extract on a small pad of cotton will keep the refrigerator fresh-smelling without a perfume odor.

Many common refrigerator odors may be removed by placing a small tub filled with charcoal in the middle rack in the refrigerator. I use the charcoal made for fish tanks.

If you are shutting off a refrigerator, be sure to prop the door open a crack for air circulation and put a container of fresh coffee grounds inside to ward off unpleasant odors. For strong odor removal, a container or nylon stocking with coffee grounds in it works wonders.

For cleaning ease, wipe the inside of the refrigerator, including shelves, with a cloth dipped in glycerin, available in the hand cream section at the drugstore. This light coating will keep spills from sticking. Even milk or sticky substances will wipe right out.

Freezers

Try using the glycerin in freezers, too. That way spills, even though frozen, wipe right out.

Wash out the freezer with a solution of 1 gallon warm water and ¼ cup borax to clean and deodorize. Rinse and dry.

Cleaning Stainless Steel Cutlery

This is such an easy way to clean your stainless steel cutlery (forks, knives, spoons). Mix the following ingredients in the kitchen sink or any nonaluminum container:

¼ cup chlorine bleach
¼ cup Calgon Water Softener®
1 gallon very hot water

Immerse stainless steel cutlery in the solution for 30 minutes and wash as usual. This is not for use on real silver.

To remove stubborn spots from stainless steel, use a little non-gel toothpaste or some silver polish in a separate container with a little ammonia added to it. Apply this with a soft cloth; wash, rinse and dry.

Cleaning Silver Cutlery

Wash silver cutlery as soon as possible after using. This prevents tarnish-causing stains. To clean a lot of silver cutlery quickly:

Put strips of aluminum foil in a large bowl. Place the silver cutlery on top. Cover the cutlery with boiling water and add 3 tablespoons of baking soda.

Soak for 10 minutes, rinse and dry. Use care on hollow or glued pieces. Also works on silver jewelry.

You can also make your own silver-cleaning cloths. Saturate cotton squares in a solution of:

2 parts ammonia

1 part silver polish

10 parts cold water

Let cloths drip dry and use as silver polish cloths.

Stainless Steel Sinks

So much of my mail asks about cleaning and keeping up the appearance of stainless steel sinks. One such writer suggested using the sink as an ugly planter and using nothing but paper plates and plastic silverware! Take heart—here are ways to keep them clean and actually enjoy them.

Regular cleaning

Clean with a paste of baking soda and water and rinse well. Drying the sink helps to prevent water marks and rust.

Polishing

Polish with flour. Put a tablespoon of flour in a dry sink and rub with a soft cloth. Then rinse and dry. Another polish method is club soda. Put the stopper in the sink, pour in some club soda and rub with a soft cloth. Again, dry to prevent water spots.

Removing rust and water spots

Use white vinegar on a soft cloth or sponge. It will not only erase the spots, but will also brighten the sink.

Rubbing alcohol or lighter fluid will also remove rust marks. Remember the flammability of lighter fluid and use with care.

Removing stains

Prepare a paste of 3 parts of cream of tartar to 1 part hydrogen peroxide and apply it to the stains. Allow it to dry and then wipe with a wet cloth or sponge.

To shine

Coat the sink with a few drops of baby oil. Wipe it off with paper towels. If it doesn't seem shiny enough, repeat the procedure.

Erasing hairline scratches

Using very fine steel wool, gently give the entire sink the once-over to obliterate hairline scratches. Then wash and buff with a soft cloth.

Metal Cleaners

Here are some fast, easy, homemade metal cleaners. Always test in an inconspicuous spot before using.

Brass

Use a mixture of lemon juice and salt. Wipe on until clean, then rinse and dry. Not for use on brass-plated pieces.

Copper

Use ketchup or Worcestershire sauce. Wipe on, rub until clean, rinse and buff.

Gold

On small pieces use non-gel toothpaste and a soft brush, such as a toothbrush. Rinse well. Any household ammoniated cleaner mixed 50/50 with water also works well.

Chrome

Rub with aluminum foil wrapped around your finger or hand, or wipe with a dry, used dryer fabric softener sheet.

USING YOUR MARBLES

When using your double boiler, drop several marbles in with the water. If it should start to boil dry, the marbles will rattle, alerting you to the problem before the pan is ruined.

The Queen's Best Kitchen Quick Tips

To remove food odors from plastic containers, fill with warm water and add a little dry mustard—¼ teaspoon is plenty for an average-size container. Let soak for an hour or so and then wash.

• To remove stains from plastic, put the open container in the sun. For stubborn spots, brush with a little lemon juice first.

• To chase away the odor of burned foods, boil some lemon slices or 1 tablespoon of bottled lemon juice in a saucepan for a few minutes.

• To chase away the odor of fried foods, even fish, place a small bowl of white vinegar next to the stove as you are frying.

• Clean porcelain pieces and the sink by filling the sink with warm water and adding several denture-cleaning tablets.

• Remove stains from the countertop by massaging a paste of cream of tartar and lemon juice into the stain, let it soak and then rinse.

• Clean and sanitize your sponge and dishcloth by wedging them into the dishwasher and washing them along with a load of dishes. You can also wet the sponge or dishcloth and put it in the microwave for 30 seconds.

• To remove grease from wooden cupboards, apply a very thin coat of car wax, let it dry and buff.

• Do not wash silver and stainless steel together in the dishwasher. The stainless may stain the silver.

• Remove plastic stuck to toasters with a little nail polish remover. Be sure toaster is unplugged.

• Store your steel wool pad in the freezer each time you finish with it and it will never rust. Just tuck it into a sandwich bag.

• To clean a scorched pan, fill with warm water and add several tablespoons of baking soda. Boil until the scorched parts loosen and float to the surface.

• Remove rust from baking pans by rubbing with cleanser and a cut raw potato.

• Spray a grater with nonstick cooking spray before using and cleanup will be a breeze.

- Clean the outside of a cast-iron pan with oven cleaner. Clean the inside by boiling a solution of water and a couple of tablespoons of white vinegar in it. Re-season with cooking oil and store with a piece of wax paper in it after each use. Never wash the inside of the pan with soap.

- To clean the inside of a thermos, fill with warm water and add 1 teaspoon of chlorine bleach. Let soak 30-60 minutes and rinse well.

- Preserve wooden salad bowls by wiping with a paper towel soaked in cooking oil. This prevents drying and cracking. Do not immerse in water for more than just a few seconds to clean. Always dry thoroughly.

- Remove rust from a knife or other kitchen utensil by sticking it in an onion for about an hour. Move the piece back and forth to help the onion juice do its work.

- Always put glass dishes into hot water sideways and they will never break from the expansion and contraction.

LAST THOUGHT

If you or someone in your family has asthma or allergies, you know the horror of opening cleaning products and having an attack. Try a new product from a company called Soapworks. They have a line of products created by a woman in direct response to her son's asthma attacks, which occurred every time she opened cleaning products and started to clean. The product is called At Home All-Purpose Cleaner™. It can be used undiluted for heavy jobs, such as degreasing, or diluted 100/1 for light cleaning. Totally safe, user- and earth-friendly, mildly scented and it works! Check out www.soapworks.com for information on their line of fabulous products.

3

Cleaning Products You Should Never Be Without

There are five cleaning products you should never be without, and most of them are things you already have in your home. You can purchase generous-size containers of all of them for a total of $10 and they will last for months. They can be used alone, together or in conjunction with other common household products such as salt or dishwashing liquid to help you handle most of the cleaning problems in your home. They are especially good for people with allergies and those of us who want to cut back on the chemicals in our homes.

HERE'S YOUR SHOPPING LIST ....

    White Vinegar
    Baking Soda
    Lemon Juice
    Club Soda
    Spot Shot Instant Carpet Stain Remover®

Now we'll take them in order and talk about their many uses.

White Vinegar

Use white vinegar to remove heavy soap scum and mineral deposits from showers, tubs and sinks. Warm the vinegar and put in a spray bottle. Spray on showers, tubs and sinks and let soak for 10-15 minutes. Then use a nylon scrubbing sponge to remove scum. Respray if necessary. To remove mineral deposits from around drains, close drain and pour in enough white vinegar to cover the drain area. Let soak overnight, scrub with a nylon scrubbing sponge, drain vinegar and rinse.

    To remove scum and mineral buildup from shower heads and keep them free-flowing, put undiluted white vinegar in a plastic bag. Tie around the shower head overnight. Scrub head and poke any loosened mineral deposits with a toothpick, rinse and enjoy your next shower.

To remove soap scum and mildew from plastic shower curtains and liners, fill the washing machine with warm water, 1 cup of white vinegar and your regular laundry detergent. Add the curtains, along with several old, light-colored towels. Run through complete cycle and rehang curtain immediately.

Add 2-3 tablespoons white vinegar to hot water along with your regular dishwashing liquid to cut grease on dishes and crystal.

Add ¼ cup of white vinegar to the washing machine during the final rinse to soften clothes and remove lint from dark clothes.

Apply, undiluted, to the skin with a cotton ball to deter bugs—they hate the way you taste, but the odor disappears immediately from your skin.

Neutralize pet urine odor with diluted white vinegar (25 percent vinegar to 75 percent water) sprayed on carpets. Always test in an inconspicuous spot before treating a large area.

Clean stainless steel sinks with a paste of baking soda and vinegar. Don't let the foaming scare you—it works great!

Make a window cleaner in a spray bottle with ¼ cup white vinegar added to 1 quart of water.

Make air freshener in a spray bottle with 1 teaspoon of baking soda, 1 tablespoon of white vinegar and 2 cups of water. After the foaming stops, put on lid. Shake before using.

Clean vinyl floors with ½ cup white vinegar to 1 gallon of warm water.

Keep drains free-flowing with ½ cup baking soda and ½ cup white vinegar poured down the drain on a monthly basis.

After pouring in baking soda and vinegar, cover the drain for 15 minutes (it will foam). Then flush with cold water.

Clean mirrors with a solution of half vinegar and half water. Wet a sponge, soft cloth or paper towel, wash and then buff dry. Never spray water onto a mirror. Moisture that gets into the edges and behind mirrors ruins the silvering on the mirror, resulting in dark spots.

Spray vinegar on the underarms of clothes and let soak 15-30 minutes to deodorize and minimize underarm stains.

Make an excellent toilet cleaner with 1 cup borax and 1 cup vinegar. Pour the vinegar over the stained area of the toilet, then sprinkle the borax over the vinegar. Soak for 2 hours and then brush and flush.

Baking Soda

Baking soda is a great deodorizer, cleaner and mild abrasive. Use as you would a soft-scrubbing product or cleanser in tubs and sinks.

Keep food disposals fresh and free-flowing by putting the stopper in the disposal and adding 3 inches of warm water and a handful of baking soda. Turn on the disposal and let water run out.

Remove perspiration stains and odor from clothing by applying a paste of baking soda and water and letting it soak 30 minutes prior to laundering.

Mix 1 gallon of warm water and ¼ cup of baking soda. Soak freshly washed socks in this for 30 minutes. Spin out in the washer (do not rinse out the solution), dry and you will have odor-eater socks.

Clean smudges on wallpaper with baking soda and water.

Remove crayon from hard surfaces with baking soda on a damp rag.

Use on any hard surface as a mild abrasive to remove stains.

Use as a bug killer for aphids. Use 1½ teaspoons of baking soda per pint of water and apply every 7 days.

To clean grout (any color), mix 3 cups of baking soda with 1 cup of warm water. Scrub grout with a brush and rinse.

Use baking soda on a damp cloth to polish silver.

To remove burnt food in casseroles, fill dish with hot water and add 1 tablespoon of baking soda and allow to soak.

To clean up pet vomit, sprinkle on a heavy coating of baking soda. Let it absorb moisture and dry, then scoop or vacuum up. The baking soda will neutralize acids and help prevent stains. Follow with Spot Shot Instant Carpet Stain Remover®.

Remove heel marks from hard floors with a damp cloth and baking soda.

Clean screen stain and mineral deposits off of windows by dipping a soft wet cloth in baking soda and rubbing gently. Follow by washing windows as usual.

Remove streaks and greasy film from car windshields with a thin paste of baking soda and water. Rinse well.

Put in the bottom of cat litter boxes to help eliminate odor. Put in a thin layer of baking soda and then add the litter as usual. This works with clay or clumping varieties.

Lemon Juice

Lemon juice is nature's bleach and disinfectant.

Apply to clothes, undiluted, to remove fruit-based stains. Let soak 30 minutes and then launder.

Remove rust from clothes by applying undiluted lemon juice and laying the garment in the sun. It disappears like magic.

Bleach spots off Formica™ counters by using straight or mixing in a paste with baking soda.

Clean brass and copper with lemon juice and salt. Sprinkle salt on a half-lemon and rub metal, then rinse thoroughly. If you don't have fresh lemons, you can also mix bottled lemon juice and salt.

Make a cleaner in a spray bottle with 2 cups of water, 2 tablespoons of lemon juice, ½ teaspoon of liquid dish soap, 1 tablespoon of baking soda and 1 teaspoon of borax. Shake before using to clean any hard surface.

Apply lemon juice to chrome and buff to a shine.

As a bleach alternative, use ¼ cup of lemon juice and ¼ cup of white vinegar mixed in 1 gallon of warm water and soak clothes for 15 minutes prior to washing.

Remove stains from hands with lemon juice.

Bleach wooden breadboards by applying lemon juice and letting it sit overnight. Wash and rinse in the morning.

Club Soda

Club soda is the best emergency spotter there is. Keep club soda on hand to clean up spills on carpet and clothing. Remember to react as soon as possible to a spill. If you act fast, a spot shouldn't become a stain. Club soda will remove red wine,

coffee, tea, pop (yes, even red pop!), Kool-Aid™ and any other spills you can think of. Lift any solids carefully off of carpet or clothes and then pour on the club soda, blotting with an old rag until all the color from the spill is removed. Don't be afraid to really wet the carpet, it won't hurt it—carpet goes through countless dippings in water as it is made. Blot carpet easily by folding a rag and standing on it, turning the rag as it absorbs moisture and discoloration from the spill. The carbonation in the club soda brings the offending spill to the surface so that you can blot it up, and the salts in it will help prevent staining.

If you spill on your clothes in a restaurant, ask for a little club soda or seltzer and use your napkin to blot the stain until it is removed. At home you can pour the club soda directly onto the spot, flushing it out.

I have found that club soda will even work on many old stains, too. Always keep several bottles on hand.

Spot Shot Instant Carpet Stain Remover®

Every home needs a good all-purpose carpet stain remover. Skip the kinds that foam, dry and you vacuum up; they leave residue in the carpet that attracts dirt. Spot Shot Instant Carpet Stain Remover® has never failed me in years of cleaning. It effectively removes water- and oil-based stains. Use it on pet stains, lipstick, makeup, hair dye, food spills, mystery spots—even old spots. Follow the label directions and you will be amazed at how well it works. It's inexpensive and available at grocery stores, Target, Wal-Mart™ and hardware stores. Make sure you have a can on hand for emergencies. It works great in conjunction with the club soda method discussed above.

4
Rust Never Sleeps

Professional rust removers are readily available at grocery stores, home centers and hardware stores. Some of them are for use only on white clothes and others can be used on colored fabrics, too. If you are using one of these chemical products, be sure to read the directions very carefully to avoid failure. If you want to remove rust from clothes with a natural, easy method and avoid chemicals, here are two ideas.

Removing Rust from Clothes

Apply lemon juice and let the item dry in the sun, then launder as usual. This is generally safe on all washable fabrics, but if in doubt try first in an inconspicuous place. Another method is to apply cream of tartar to the rust spot, gather up the edges of the material and dip the spot into hot water. Let it sit for 5 minutes and then launder as usual.

To Remove Rust from Metal

Sprinkle scouring powder on a cork, then rub the stain. Wash and rinse as usual.

To Remove Rust from Fixtures

Rub the rust spot with salt and lemon juice until the rust disappears. Then rinse and polish.

To Remove Rust from the Toilet Bowl

There are, of course, acid bowl cleaners available from grocery stores, home centers and janitorial supply stores that will remove rust from toilets, but for an inexpensive, nontoxic way to remove rust, try this: Once a month sprinkle a layer of Tang™ Breakfast Drink or lemon Kool-Aid™ on the sides of the toilet and in the water, leave for an hour, brush and flush. Repeat if necessary. (For those of you who are wondering, citric acid oxidizes the rust.)

To Remove Rust from Stainless Steel Sinks

Rub the rust spot with lighter fluid until the rust is removed, and then follow up with liquid cleaner. Be careful when you do this not to work around an open flame, and be sure you have the area ventilated adequately.

To Remove Rust from Utensils

This is a great, easy tip—try it the next time you're making a salad! Stick the utensils, such as knives, forks, etc., into an onion. Pull back and forth on the utensil and then let it sit there so the onion juice can do its job.

To Remove Rust from Chrome

This tip works great on car chrome. Take a crumpled ball of aluminum foil and rub the rust spot until it disappears.

To Remove Rust from Countertops

This works on Formica™, plastic laminates, etc. Make a paste of cream of tartar and either lemon juice or hydrogen peroxide, apply to the rust spot and allow to sit for about 30 minutes. Scrub with nylon-type scrubbing sponge and rinse. If necessary, reapply.

5

Taming Dust Bunnies Without a Whip

Dusting is one of those thankless jobs that we all have to do. No matter how many times we do it, we still have to do it again and again. These are things that you can do to make the job easier and faster.

Home-Treated Dust Cloths

There are many dusting products on the market that you can buy, but you can easily make your own treated dust cloths for just pennies. Here's how:

Use your favorite cleaning product to make up a bucket of hot, sudsy water. Add a couple of teaspoons of turpentine. Throw in some clean, cotton dust cloths, stir so that they get saturated, and let them soak for 8 to 10 hours (I usually leave them overnight). After they have soaked, wring them out and air-dry them. As soon as they are dry they are ready to use.

Mix together two cups of hot water and one cup of lemon oil. Dip lint-less cloths into the solution. Squeeze thoroughly and air-dry. Store in a covered metal can—an old coffee can works great.

Lambswool Dusters

For dusting hard-to-reach and high areas, use a good lambswool duster. Do not use a feather duster; it simply shifts the dust around. A lambswool duster attracts dust, is easily washed and can be used for years. Look for these at janitorial supply stores, home centers, in mail-order catalogs and websites that sell cleaning supplies.

Dust Repellent

To keep dust off blinds, refrigerators and glass-top tables, mix a solution of 1 part liquid fabric softener to 4 parts water. Spray on or apply with a soft cloth and dry with a soft cloth. This will repel the dust.

Dusting Prints

Use cornstarch to remove extra furniture polish and wipe off fingerprints on wood furniture. Shake a little on the surface and polish with a soft cloth.

6

Floor Cleaning—
Now Step on It

Once you know a few basics you can clean your floors quickly and easily—just like the pros.

Sealing Ceramic Tile

Sealing your grout is a must. Purchase sealer from the store where you bought your tile or from a home center.

Cleaning Ceramic Tile

Ceramic tile is not porous—you can clean effectively with warm water. Many cleaners leave a residue on the tile surface that looks like a smeary coating. A good neutral cleaner for tile is 1 gallon warm water, 2 tablespoons of ammonia and 1 tablespoon of borax. Never use vinegar. It is acidic and will eventually etch the grout.

Never use a sponge mop on ceramic tile. It works like a squeegee, depositing the dirty water into the grout tracks.

Sweep or vacuum floor prior to washing.

Use a rag or chamois-type mop.

Rinse mop, frequently changing the water as it becomes soiled.

If you have a gloss-finish tile it may be necessary to dry the tile. Use a clean terry rag under your foot to do it the easy way.

Dusting Wood Floors

Use a dry dust mop to remove dust or vacuum floor, being sure not to use a vacuum with a beater bar—this can mar the floor.

Cleaning Wood Floors with Tea

Tea is a wonderful cleaner for wood because of the tannic acid. Brew 1 quart of boiling water with 1 or 2 tea bags. Let it come to room temperature. Wring out a soft cloth to just damp and wash floor, keeping the rag clean. Do not over-wet floor. This will clean the floor and cover many imperfections. Buff with a soft cloth if desired.

Repair Scratches in Wood Floors

To fill scratches, use a crayon or combine several to match the floor. Wax crayons for wood are available at the hardware store. Work the crayon into the scratch, then heat the repair with a blow-dryer and buff with a rag. This will work the repair into the floor so well, you'll never know it's there.

Clean and Wax

There is a product made by Bruce Floor Care Products that is a cleaner and wax in one. It comes in two colors, light and dark. If your floors are very bad you might consider trying this product before you spend the money to refinish the floors. Follow the directions on the can carefully, and allow plenty of time to do the job, working in one small area at a time.

Cleaning Vinyl Floors

For cleaning vinyl floors, including no-wax floors, sheet vinyl and linoleum:

Sweep or vacuum the floor well. Mix 1 gallon of warm water and 1 tablespoon of borax. Wring out mop or rag well in the solution and wash the floor, keeping the rag clean. No rinsing is necessary. Using borax preserves the shine on floors, even those that have been waxed.

Waxing Floors

When you wax a floor it is wise to buy the wax from a janitorial store, which sells commercial products that hold up well to wear and traffic.

On a clean floor apply 2 thin coats of wax, allowing ample drying time between coats. It is imperative that the floor be clean, otherwise you will wax in the dirt.

The next time you wax, wax only the traffic area where the wax is worn off, feathering it into the other areas to blend. This eliminates wax buildup around the edges of the room.

Purchase a wax-stripping product from your local janitorial supply store. It is more efficient than ammonia and also very reasonably priced.

The Miracle of Microfiber . . . or Is It?

Microfiber cloths and mops clean without chemicals—just water and the cloth or mop. Do these products work? Well . . . yes and no. The old adage *you get what you pay for* certainly holds true in the microfiber business. If you are purchasing these cloths dirt cheap you are wasting your money. If they do not contain thousands of fibers, they won't clean as they should. Here's the dirty lowdown on the very best.

Euronet USA makes the Act Natural Mop™. A dry mop/wet mop with a telescoping handle, this miracle cleans vinyl, ceramic, wood—any hard flooring—beautifully with nothing but water. Just wring the mop out in water, stick it to the velcro pad and go! Machine wash. Check out www.euronetusa.com or call 888-638-2882.

7

Today's Wood— Tomorrow's Heirlooms

Wood furniture in a home is a big investment. Properly cared for, it will last and keep its new appearance for years, eventually to be called "antique" by our grandchildren and great-grandchildren. Here are some tips to keep your furniture looking great, some tips on fixing problems that arise, plus the recipe for making your own furniture polish.

Making Your Own Furniture Polish

There are several great furniture polishes you can make at home with ease. The general rule for homemade polish is to rub it in with a soft cloth and wipe it off and buff with another clean, soft cloth.

Combine ¼ cup white vinegar and 1 cup olive oil in a clean container. Shake before each use.

Combine 1 cup of mineral oil and 3 drops of lemon extract. Shake before each use.

Grate 2 ounces of beeswax (available at drugstores) into a jar and cover it with 5 ounces of natural turpentine. Shake occasionally until dissolved, or stand in a bowl of hot water. Apply to furniture with a soft cloth (just a small amount is all that is needed) and buff with a clean, soft cloth. If it becomes hard over a period of time, set it in a bowl of hot water. This formula seems to work especially well on unvarnished furniture.

Water Marks/Heat Scars and White Rings

Massage mayonnaise into the marks and leave it on overnight. The next morning, wipe off the mayonnaise and the marks should be gone. You can also use petroleum jelly, butter or margarine. If you have a really stubborn spot, mix cigarette ashes or rottenstone (available at the hardware store) with the mayonnaise and repeat the above procedure.

Non-gel white toothpaste is also effective in removing white water rings. Dab toothpaste on a damp cloth and gently massage the ring in a circular motion until it's gone. Wipe and buff with a soft cloth. Apply furniture polish if necessary.

Remove Old Polish and Dirt

Put 2 tea bags in a pot with 1 quart of water and bring it to a boil. Cool to room temperature. Dip a soft cloth in the solution, wring it until it is just damp and wipe furniture with it. Buff it dry with a soft cloth, then decide if it requires polish.

Restoring Dried-Out Furniture

Dab petroleum jelly on a soft cloth and polish to help feed and restore dry wood. You will be amazed to see the wood grain and natural luster appear.

Cleaning Very Dirty Wood Furniture

Mix a solution of 1 quart warm water and 3 or 4 drops of dishwashing liquid. Wash the furniture with a soft cloth wrung out until it is damp, rinse and buff dry.

Covering Scratches

To cover scratches on wood furniture, use a crayon the color of the wood. Apply to the scratched area, heat with a blow-dryer and buff the crayon into the scratch with a soft cloth.

For darker woods, rub the meat of a pecan or walnut into the scratch and buff well.

To cover scratches on mahogany or cherry wood, use iodine.

Removing Stickers from Wood

To remove a price tag, identifying label or decal from wood, pull up as much of the sticker as possible, then dip a cloth in vegetable oil or baby oil and gently scrub the area until the sticker and adhesive are gone. Finish by buffing well with a soft cloth.

8

Off the Walls— Wash Them Like the Pros

Wall-washing can actually be easy if you have the right equipment and do it the right way. Here are some tips for spotting, removing marks and washing walls.

Have All the Right Stuff

When you are ready to wash walls, be sure you gather up the right things to do the job quickly and easily. Get things together before you start and have the furniture moved away from the walls so that the washing process will flow smoothly. Do it like a professional. Here is a list of the things you should have:

2 buckets
Natural sponge (not one of those awful nylon ones)
Baking soda and a soft rag
Art gum eraser
Dropcloths
Ladder
Ingredients for cleaning solution of your choice
2 strips of washcloth or terry rags and 2 rubber bands

QUICK TIP ....

Use a dropcloth on the floor around the area you will be washing—it will save you time and mess in the long run. A fabric dropcloth is preferable to plastic, as it absorbs and isn't slippery when wet. Before you start to wash, wrap a strip of washcloth or turkish toweling around your wrist several times and secure with rubber bands. This will keep drips from running up your arms when you are working with your arms above your head.

Removing Marks

The first thing you want to try to do is erase the marks on the wall away. Use an art gum eraser that you keep on hand for this purpose and erase just the mark. This works on many types of marks. If you still have some stubborn spots, use a little baking soda on the corner of a white rag and rub gently, doing just the mark. Non-gel toothpaste also is a good spot remover; use it on a cloth over the tip of your finger.

Crayon Marks

If you have kids, you have probably had crayon on the wall. To remove crayon easily, spray with WD-40™ lubricant and wipe crayon away with a paper towel. Follow up with a soft cloth and a solution of hot water and a little dishwashing liquid, washing in a circular motion.

Ink and Marker Marks

To remove ink or Magic Marker®, use hair spray (the cheaper the better), rubbing alcohol, or for really tough spots, denatured alcohol from the hardware store. Always spot carefully, trying to do just the spot.

Great Wall-Washing Solutions

Try one of these wall-washing solutions:

• 1 gallon warm water, ½ cup ammonia, ¼ cup white vinegar and ¼ cup washing soda

• 1 gallon warm water, 1 cup ammonia and 1 teaspoon mild dishwashing liquid

For really professional results, rinse the walls with clear water after washing with either of these solutions. If you choose not to rinse, then be sure to change the cleaning solution frequently as it becomes soiled.

Where to Start

You have the wall free of marks, your dropcloths are in place, your wrists are wrapped for drips and you have your washing solution ready. Now wet your natural sponge (available at janitorial supply stores, home centers and hardware stores). Don't skimp and use a nylon sponge or a rag; it will drag as you wash and take you twice as long. A natural sponge has thousands of "scrubbing fingers" and will get the job done fast, easy and right. Begin washing at the bottom of the wall and work up, doing the ceiling last. Drips of water are much easier to wipe off of a clean wall and won't leave marks like they do on a soiled wall.

Don't Stop!

Once you start on a wall, don't stop in the middle. Complete one full wall or the full ceiling before you take a break. If you stop in the middle of a wall or ceiling you will have "tide marks" where you stop and start again.

Keeping Walls Clean

You can make your own brushing tool to use between washing, to dust down the walls. Tie a clean dust cloth loosely around a broom head and use to dust ceiling thoroughly from time to time and to dust down walls. Give the broom a shake now and then as you are working to remove dust.

Grease Spots on Wallpaper

Make a paste of cornstarch and water and apply to the grease spot. Allow it to dry, then brush or vacuum it off.

Apply a double fold of brown paper (a grocery bag works well, but don't use the part with the writing on it) and press over the grease spot with a warm iron. This may require several efforts. This method also works well on candle wax. Follow up with a little hair spray or alcohol.

Removing Crayon from Wallpaper

Rub lightly with a dry soap-filled steel wool pad. Do this very gently. You can also try rubbing with baking soda on a damp cloth. On vinyl paper, try using a little silver polish.

Smudges, Marks and Mystery Stains on Wallpaper

Erase with an art gum eraser.

To remove marks from nonwashable paper: Rub a scrunched-up piece of white bread over the marks. Rub very gently. You may need to repeat this a few times before you make progress.

Washing Wallpaper

Wash vinyl and washable papers with one of the mild wall-washing solutions in this chapter.

Cloth Wall Coverings

To clean grasscloth, burlap or cloth wall covering, vacuum with the soft duster brush on the vacuum. Do this regularly to maintain the appearance.

Wood Paneling

Clean wood paneling following the suggestions in the chapter on wood floor cleaning.

9

Up, Up and Away— Upholstery Cleaning Made Easy

This chapter will give you all the information you need to choose upholstered furniture wisely, spot-clean it, handle emergency spills and clean it thoroughly.

One of the first things everyone should know about upholstery is that there are different cleaning methods for different types of fabric. There is a simple way to check to see how the furniture you have now should be cleaned, and even more importantly, how a new piece should be cleaned. This will help you make good decisions on wearability and cleanability before you get the piece home.

Cleaning Codes and What They Mean

Upholstery is supposed to be marked with a code that allows the consumer to know in advance what type of cleaning the manufacturer recommends for that particular piece of furniture. These instructions, known as cleaning codes, are generally found under the seat cushions on the platform of the furniture (the part that the cushions sit on). I will discuss each cleaning code individually below. If you do not find the code under the seat cushions, check all tags for instructions and never buy any upholstered furniture without knowing how it can be cleaned. This information is essential.

W

If you find a W on your furniture, it means that it can be cleaned with water. This would mean that you could rent an extraction carpet and upholstery cleaning machine from the home center or hardware store or use one that you have purchased to clean the fabric. You can also use water in spotting spills. This is the most durable and cleanable fabric you can buy. It is ideal for dining chairs, family room furniture, anything that gets heavy use or where spills might occur frequently.

S

If you find an S on your furniture, it means that it must be cleaned with cleaning solvents (dry-clean only) and you cannot apply water to it. This would eliminate spot-cleaning with water-based products. Dry-clean only fabrics are generally not as durable and also do not clean as well. If you have a piece with this code, do not allow it to become heavily soiled before calling in a professional cleaner or you will be disappointed with the results. If you need to spot-clean a dry-clean only fabric, try using Energine Cleaning Fluid®, available at grocery and hardware stores. Test it first in an inconspicuous spot to be sure it doesn't damage the fabric. Apply with a clean, light-colored cloth and blot continuously. Once you have removed the spot, use a blow-dryer to dry the spot quickly so it doesn't leave a noticeable ring on the fabric.

S/W

This code means a combination of solvents and water can be used to clean the upholstery. It does not appear on many pieces. It is best left to the professionals to clean this. Use furniture with this code in low-use areas.

X

This code does not appear on furniture as much any more, but it does appear frequently on fabric blinds and shades. It means that the item is not cleanable and is a vacuum-only piece. Beware!

Don't Undress Your Furniture

Many people have asked me about taking the covers off the foam cushions and washing them in the washing machine—DON'T DO IT! The zippers are in the backs of cushions only so that the foam cushions may be changed by a professional if necessary. If you remove the cushion covers and wash them they may shrink and not fit back on the foam correctly; no matter what, it is virtually impossible to get them back on the foam forms evenly and correctly. Plus, they will be noticeably cleaner than the rest of the sofa and will fade and wear out more quickly.

Spot Cleaning

If you need to spot-clean a cushion, unzip the zipper and put a pad of paper towels or a folded white rag between the foam and the cushion covering. Apply your spotter, carefully following the directions. Try not to rub the area, as it causes abrasion on the fabric surface—BLOT - BLOT - BLOT. I have had great success with Spot Shot Upholstery Stain Remover®. It is easy to use and works on a wide variety of spills and soiling. It can be used on a wide variety of fabrics (always test any spotter in an inconspicuous area before using) and works well on the sofa or chair body as well as the cushions. It is great for food spills on dining chairs. Remember, whatever spotting method you choose, always first do a test area where it won't show.

Candle Wax Meets Upholstery

If you have the unfortunate accident of having candle wax come in contact with your upholstery, don't despair. First, put a large quantity of ice in a plastic bag and lay it on the wax long enough to allow the wax to freeze. Remove the ice and immediately chip up any wax that you can.

Next, take a brown grocery bag and, using only the part without writing, lay it over the wax. Using a medium/hot iron, press over the wax, allowing it to absorb into the paper bag. Move the bag continuously to a clean area. Once you have absorbed as much of the wax as possible, use Energine Cleaning Fluid® to spot-clean the area, remembering to use a blow-dryer to dry the spot when you are done.

If any staining remains, use 3 percent hydrogen peroxide from the drugstore applied with a spoon to bleach out the wax color. Apply peroxide, wait 15 minutes and blot, continuing until the color from the wax is gone.

⑩ Leather Report

Many of us have leather furniture, car interiors, clothes and accessories. Unfortunately, along with wearing leather and using it in our homes comes the frustration of cleaning it.

Cleaning Leather Furniture

Keep leather furniture out of direct sunlight, otherwise it may crack and dry out. You should use hide food once or twice a year to ensure that the leather remains supple. Make sure you rub it in well so that it does not come off on clothes. I like to apply it, rub it in well, let it sit for 12 hours and then buff again before using the piece. Dust or vacuum regularly and clean with saddle soap or wipe with a damp cloth rubbed across a wet bar of glycerin soap or moisturizing facial soap, such as Dove. If the leather piece is tufted and has buttons and piping, use a soft, bristled toothbrush or paintbrush moistened and rubbed across the soap. Always dry leather with a clean, lint-free cloth.

If you have a sealed leather table or desktop, clean, polish and seal it with paste wax once or twice a year.

Leather Apparel

If you have dirty leather shoes, purses, coats or accessories, you can treat them much the same way that you do your furniture. For cleaning purses and shoes, a damp, soft cloth rubbed across a bar of moisturizing facial soap, such as Dove, works well. You should always use care to not over-wet the article. Do not rinse after washing; instead, allow to dry naturally, then polish as usual.

Water Spots

Simply run a damp sponge over the area and allow to dry.

Salt Stains

Dab on a solution of 3 parts white vinegar to 1 part water.

Ink Stains and Spots

To remove ink stains and spots from leather, apply a little cuticle remover. Dab it on the spot and rub gently with a soft cloth, wipe and buff. You may need to allow the cuticle remover to sit for 10 minutes or so before rubbing for difficult stains. Reapply if necessary.

Dark Stains

If you have light-colored leather furniture and apparel with dark stains on it, try wiping gently with a thin paste of lemon juice and cream of tartar. Gently massage in, then finish off with a soft damp cloth. Be sure to rinse well and follow up with one of the cleaning methods above.

Removing Mildew

To remove mildew from leather, apply a coat of petroleum jelly, allow to sit for 4-5 hours and then rub off.

Making Hide Food

Make your own "hide food" by mixing 1 part vinegar to 2 parts linseed oil in a jar with a lid. Shake well and apply with a soft cloth, changing it frequently as it soils. Buff well so oil won't transfer to clothes. Test in an inconspicuous area before using on light-colored leather.

11

Meticulous Marble— Leave No Stone Unturned

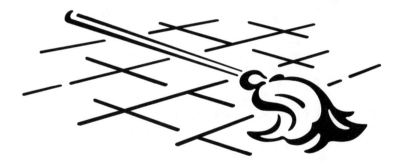

While bathroom and kitchen countertops are usually synthetic (cultured marble), marble used in living room and other furniture is usually the genuine article. Seal it with a stone sealer because it is very susceptible to stains, and wipe up spills quickly.

Maintaining Marble

Dust and/or wipe with a damp cloth as needed. Caked-on spots can be sprinkled with borax or baking powder and rubbed with a damp sponge or cloth. You can also use a commercial marble polish.

Bathroom or kitchen marble can be cleaned with ⅓ liquid fabric softener to ⅔ water. Clean thoroughly and polish with a soft cloth.

Fine Scratches

Use extra-fine steel wool to apply baking soda and water mixed to a paste. Flush with water and let it dry; repeat if necessary. Buff with a dry cloth or use a buffing wheel on your electric drill.

Grease Stains

These are circular and often dark in the center. Wash surface with ammonia, rinse with plenty of water, then repeat—OR, cover area with a ½-inch-thick paste of 20 percent hydrogen peroxide and powdered whiting from the paint store. Keep it damp by covering it with plastic wrap sealed with masking tape. After 10-15 minutes, rinse with water, avoiding any wood trim. Repeat if necessary. Buff and then polish.

Rust

Rub with a rough cloth or make a mix of commercial liquid rust remover and whiting and follow the directions for grease stains. After removing the paste, rub marble with dry cloth.

Tea, Coffee, Ink

Use hydrogen peroxide/whiting method—see grease stains method.

Water

Use hydrogen peroxide, applied with a medicine dropper, followed with a drop or two of household ammonia. After 20 minutes, wash area.

Wine

Use hydrogen peroxide.

Mystery Stains

To remove stains of an unknown origin, try hydrogen peroxide mixed with cream of tartar or non-gel toothpaste, rubbed in with a soft cloth and rinsed off.

Restoring the Polish

To restore the polish to marble, rub with a cloth dampened with turpentine.

Warm Up That Spot

Warming marble with a blow-dryer or setting the object in the sun will make the stain removal work more quickly.

12

The Queen's Royal Carpet Treatment

Carpet is one of the most expensive investments you will make in your home. With proper knowledge about choosing a good-quality carpet that fits your lifestyle, and cleaning and stain removal guidelines, your carpet will give you many years of enjoyment and quality wear.

Know Your Carpet

Most residential carpet is made from one of four fibers: nylon, polyester, olefin or wool (or a combination). All of these fibers can make great carpet, although nylon is one of the most cost-effective and durable. Here are some other things to be aware of when making that important purchase.

Face Weight is a common-sense measurement that you should be aware of when purchasing carpet. The key to remember: More fibers are almost always better.

Fiber Density is a measurement of how closely packed carpet fibers are to each other. Carpets with high density tend to look better longer and will give carpet a soft feeling when walked upon.

Carpet Fiber Twist is very important to be aware of, especially with cut-pile types of carpet. Fibers that have more twists per linear inch usually make more durable carpeting.

Carpet Padding is absolutely critical to good carpet performance. Too much or too little can cause premature failure in many carpets. The best pads, believe it or not, are those that are thin and firm. Avoid pads thicker than 7/16 inch.

Cleaning Carpet

Many people ask me how to go about hiring a firm to clean carpeting. Listed below are some general guidelines to follow. Always call more than one company, looking for comparable pricing. Ask each company the same set of questions, and remember word-of-mouth is one of your best allies. Ask your neighbors, your friends, the people you work with which companies they have used and how satisfied they were.

QUESTIONS TO ASK

Cost Per Square Foot or Room

Find out if there is a square footage limitation per room and if your room sizes fit within the limitation. Remember to ask about hallways, walk-in closets and bathrooms. They may count as a whole room when companies offer room pricing. If the cost is figured by square foot, measure the length and width of your rooms and multiply length by width to achieve the square footage. Add the total square footage of all of your rooms and multiply by the cost per square foot. This should give you an accurate price.

Find Out What Method of Cleaning Is Used

Steam cleaning or extraction is the preferable way to clean. Ask if the company uses a "truck mounted unit." A portable cleaner will not generate the same powerful extraction process that a truck unit will.

Do They Clean with Hot or Cold Water?

Cold water will not remove stubborn, greasy soil. A truck-mounted cleaning system should hook up to your cold water, usually at an outside tap, and heat the water as it flows through the truck.

Is the Company Insured?

If they damage your furniture while moving it or bang

into a wall, you want to be sure they can cover the cost of the repair.

Ask About Experience

Be sure you are hiring trained professionals who do this for a living.

Remember the Investment

Again, carpet is one of your most expensive investments, so treat it with the care it deserves and it will last much longer and look better.

Before Cleaning Carpets

- Pick up all small items from carpets.

- Remove all items from furniture to be moved.

- When possible, remove dining chairs and other small, light pieces of furniture.

- Pick up all small area rugs.

- Remove things from the floor of the closet if it will be cleaned.

- Remove anything from under beds if they are to be moved.

- Open as many windows as possible, if weather permits.

- If house is not left open, turn on the air conditioner or heat, whichever is appropriate.

- If possible, set fans so they blow across the carpet.

• Wash the soles of the shoes or slippers that you will be wearing on the damp carpet, otherwise dirt from the soles will be transferred to the carpet.

• Do not move furniture back until carpet is completely dry.

After Carpets Are Cleaned

BEWARE of slippery linoleum and other hard floors when stepping from damp carpet.

• Do not put towels or sheets or newspapers on the carpet.

• If you have had the carpet treated with carpet protector, you will need to allow extra drying time.

• Vacuum carpet thoroughly after it is dry with a clean vacuum.

Spotting Guide

The number one rule of spot removal on carpet is to always keep several bottles of club soda on hand to use on spills on any kind of carpet. If you spill, follow this advice:

Blot up as much moisture as you can—laying old towels over the spill and standing on them is a great way to start.

• Scrape up any solids.

• Pour club soda on the spill. Don't be afraid to really pour it on. The carbonation in the soda will "bubble up" the spill so that you can blot it up. Again, cover the spot with clean, light-colored towels or rags and stand on them. This will really help to absorb the spill. Continue to pour and absorb until all color from the stain has been blotted up and the towel is coming up clean.

• Follow up with a good carpet stain remover. I prefer Spot Shot Instant Carpet Stain Remover®.

• When you spot-clean carpet, never rub, as it will only spread the stain and will cause abrasion to the carpet fibers.

• This is a good general cleaning method for most spills and definitely will not cause any damage.

Red Pop, Kool-Aid™

Grab the club soda fast and follow the above method. If the stain is old, still try the club soda—it will help lighten the stain. After using your carpet spotter, if the spot is still present, saturate with hydrogen peroxide or undiluted lemon juice. Wait 15 minutes and blot. Continue to apply and check your progress, just to be sure you aren't lightening the carpet.

Red Wine

Grab the white wine and pour it on or saturate with salt and follow with the club soda and carpet spotter.

Nail Polish

Blot up as much polish as possible with a tissue or anything handy. Then test the effect of nonoily nail polish remover on an inconspicuous part of the carpet. If there are no ill effects to the carpet pile, apply the nail polish remover with an eye dropper or a nonsilver spoon, blotting immediately after each application. Always use nonoily polish remover. If regular nail polish remover does not work, buy straight acetone at a beauty supply house, pretest again, and apply as directed above. Once you have removed as much as possible (have patience) follow with Spot Shot Carpet Stain Remover®, applied according to the directions. If color staining remains, apply hydrogen peroxide to bleach or lighten the stain.

Mud

Cover wet mud with salt or baking soda and let dry thoroughly before touching. Once it is dry, vacuum it using the attachment hose to concentrate the suction on the mud. Use a good carpet spotter, following the directions, to complete the process. For red dirt or mud, use a rust remover such as Whink® or Rust Magic® to remove any color residue. Make sure you test the rust remover in a small area first.

Coffee and Tea

The best defense is a good offense when you spill coffee. First, act as quickly as possible. Hot coffee is the equivalent of brown dye. Blot up all of the spill that you can and immediately apply club soda. If you don't have club soda (shame on you), use plain cold water. Really pour it on and blot, blot, blot. Follow with a good-quality carpet spotter. If a stain remains you can attempt to remove it by pouring on hydrogen peroxide, waiting 15 minutes and then blotting. If it is lightening the stain, continue and as a final step rinse with cold water or club soda.

Use Shaving Cream

The great instant spot remover! If you have a spill and have no carpet spotter available, grab the shaving cream. It is particularly effective on makeup, lipstick, coffee and tea. Work it into the spot well and rinse with either cold water or club soda.

Guide to Special Spots

Spots Such as Tar and Mustard

Work glycerin (available at drugstores in the hand cream section) into the spot. Let it sit 30-60 minutes. Working carefully with paper towels, use a lifting motion to remove the spot. This may require multiple treatments. Follow with a good spotter, such as Spot Shot®.

Removing Indentations in Carpet

Lay ice cubes in the indentations caused by furniture. Be sure to cover all of the indented area. Leave overnight and then fluff the nap with the tines of a fork the next day.

Candle Wax

Put ice in a plastic bag and lay over the wax, allowing it to freeze. Chip off all wax that you can. Next, lay brown paper over the wax (a grocery bag works great; use the area without the writing) and press with a medium/hot iron. Move the paper as it absorbs so that you don't redeposit the wax on the carpet. Have patience and continue as long as any wax shows up on the bag. Next, apply a good carpet stain remover.

Soot

Sprinkle with salt and wait at least 2 hours and then vacuum, using the attachment hose to concentrate the suction. Spot with a good spotter or Energine Cleaning Fluid®.

Gum

Freeze with ice in a bag and chip off all that you can. Work a little petroleum jelly into the remaining residue and roll the gum into it. Scrape up and follow with a good spotter or Energine Cleaning Fluid®.

Glue

Try saturating glue with undiluted white vinegar. Working with an upward motion, work it out of the fibers and spot with Energine Cleaning Fluid®. For rubber cement, use the method above for gum.

Ink

Spray on hair spray or blot with rubbing alcohol. For heavy spots, try denatured alcohol. Blot well and follow with a spotter.

Armed for Battle

Always keep a good carpet spotting product on hand! I have found an incredible product that removes not only fresh red stains, but also old ones. It will work effectively on such things as red wine, red pop, Kool-Aid™, cranberry juice, red food coloring and even black coffee and tea. It is called Wine Away Red Wine Stain Remover™. Don't let the name fool you, if you are a mom you need this product, if you drink red wine you need it too! It is totally nontoxic and works on carpet and upholstery, even car seats. Call 888-WINEAWAY for a purchase location near you.

13

Are Pets Turning Your Home into a Barnyard?

Do your pets have accidents in the house? Did you have a pet-sitter while you were on a trip and the cat didn't use the litterbox and the dog didn't go outside? Do you know what to do when the cat leaves you a hairball surprise on the carpet or the spaghetti didn't agree with the dog? Help is on the way! Here's all the information you need to clean up pet accidents and keep them from happening again.

Pet Odor

Pet odor caused from urine or feces is one of the toughest deodorizing problems you will face. The stain from the problem is only a small part of the dilemma. Unless you completely deodorize the area where the pet accident occurred, the animal, especially cats, will return to the spot and resoil it.

Pet odor is a protein-based problem and cannot be eliminated by normal spotting procedures. In order to remove odor, you must use an enzyme product to digest the protein, particularly in urine. If you do not use the correct cleaning procedure, the cat or dog will locate the smell and re-use the area, since animals operate primarily on a sense of smell.

Enzyme products may be purchased at pet supply stores, veterinary clinics and janitorial supply stores. There are many enzyme products available. Two that I particularly like that are available nationwide are Outright Pet Odor Eliminator® made by the Bramton Company and Nature's Miracle®.

I have had experience with both products and find that they both work well. I tend to favor Outright because I successfully used it in my former business and personally (thanks to Zack, my 17-pound bengal cat) for 15 years.

Do not be fooled into believing that you can spray on a deodorizer and the odor will magically disappear. It won't happen, and you will have wasted time and money on a product that doesn't work. Now let's get to the basics of pet odor removal.

First, Remove and Blot

You must remove any solid waste from the area and blot up any liquid residue using a heavy pad, paper towels or old, disposable rags. Lay this pad on the carpet and stand on it to absorb as much liquid as possible.

Step Two, Treat

Now you are ready to treat the accident with the enzyme product of your choice. Read the directions on the product carefully, following them exactly. Do not be afraid to really saturate the carpet. Generally, pet accidents soak through the carpet back and into the pad, so the enzyme treatment needs to soak in just as deeply. Water will not hurt your carpet; it is dipped in water numerous times during the dyeing process. Not putting the enzyme in deeply enough will not eliminate the odor. This is the most important step, so be sure to saturate the entire area, covering the circumference of the stain thoroughly, too. Remember, the urine goes into the carpet deeply and spreads.

The Secret

Cover the treated area with a plastic garbage bag or a dry cleaner's bag. If there is any lettering on the bag do not let it touch the carpet or it will transfer to the carpet. Weight the plastic down with something heavy—the idea is to keep the enzyme from drying out until it can do its job, which is digesting the protein in the urine or feces. Leave the plastic in place at least 24 hours, preferably 48 hours—resist temptation, don't peek!

Step Three

Uncover the area and allow it to dry thoroughly. This may require as much as a week to 10 days, depending on how deeply you treated the spot. To speed drying, let a fan blow across the area.

Step Four

Once the area is completely dry (and only then), check for odor. If there is still odor, re-treat as directed above. If the odor is gone, clean the area with a good-quality carpet spotter that specializes in pet stains. I like Spot Shot Instant Carpet Stain Remover®. I have used it for years; and it works quickly and efficiently and won't leave residue in the carpet to encourage re-soiling.

If you have pets, keep some enzyme cleaner and carpet spotter on hand for pet accident emergencies.

Don't Panic If You Have No Enzyme or Carpet Spotter!

There is hope even if you don't have an enzyme product on hand. First, soak up as much liquid as possible from the carpet and remove any solids. If you have club soda on hand, pour that on and blot by standing on paper towels or rags (if you have no club soda, then use cold water). Do this repeatedly to remove as much urine as possible. Mix a mild solution of white vinegar and water (⅓ cup vinegar in a 1-quart bottle filled with cool water) in a spray bottle and spray onto pet stains to help remove the smell. Rinse with clear water and blot. Now go to the store at the earliest possible moment and buy the enzyme product and spotter and use as discussed previously.

Oops! The Carpet Changed Color

Urine spots may change the carpet color. The carpet may be lightened or bleached. Many times this is not obvious until the carpet is cleaned the first time after the accident. It is more common when the stain has not been treated in an appropriate manner. If this happens, try sponging the area with a mild ammonia solution. This will sometimes return the carpet to its original color or at least make it less noticeable.

Pet Accidents on Upholstered Furniture

When pets have accidents on upholstered furniture, you must first be sure that the fabric can be cleaned and treated with water. Check the platform of the sofa or chair under the cushion to determine the cleaning code. It should be listed on a tag. W indicates that the piece can be cleaned with water, so it can be treated as described on page 50. Clean the area using a good-quality upholstery spotting product. If the code is an S, this means solvent must be used in the cleaning process and this must be done by a professional. Do not apply an enzyme product or spotter. Call a professional. In this instance, the foam in the cushion may require replacing after cleaning.

If a pet urinates on a mattress, treat it as described on pages 70-72, but when done treating with the enzyme, cover the spot with plastic and stand the mattress on edge to expedite drying. If possible, leave the enzyme on for 12 hours.

Remove the plastic and sprinkle the area with borax. Let dry thoroughly and vacuum well. If necessary, follow by cleaning with a good-quality carpet spotter.

When the Cat Leaves You a Hairball or the Spaghetti Doesn't Agree with the Dog

If you have pets, you know what it's like when your cat or dog suffers a digestive upset. You hear the problem begin and run to move the dog or cat off the carpet (which seems to be their favorite place to leave "gifts"), but you're too late and faced with a mess to clean up.

First, resist the temptation to wipe up the mess. If there are solids that can be picked up with a paper towel, do so, but do not smear the accident into the carpet. Trying to wipe it up immediately will only make the mess worse. Instead, sprinkle a heavy coating of baking soda on the area and allow it to dry. The baking soda will absorb moisture and digestive acids. Once the area is dry, remove with paper towels or vacuum the area, removing all of the mess that will come up. Vacuum very thoroughly to remove the baking soda. Then and only then, you should grab the rag and the cleaner. Use your favorite carpet spotter, following the directions carefully. Remember to blot rather than rub.

If any discoloration remains after cleaning, try applying either undiluted lemon juice or hydrogen peroxide from the drugstore. Let it soak on the stain for 15 minutes and then blot. If the spot is still visible, apply again, watching carefully to be sure that there are no changes in carpet color. If you need a more aggressive treatment, mix lemon juice and cream of tartar into a thin paste. Apply to the spot, let dry and then vacuum up. When done with any of these procedures, rinse the carpet with cool water.

Removing Pet Hair from Fabric

Sometimes the vacuum cleaner isn't enough to remove pet hair from upholstered furniture. If this is true in your case, try one of the following methods:

• Dampen a sponge and wipe over the furniture, rinsing the sponge as necessary.

• Wipe down with your hands while wearing rubber gloves.

• Wrap tape around hands and wipe, changing as needed.

• Wipe with dampened body-washing puff.

• Wipe with a used dryer fabric softener sheet.

Keeping Cats from Digging in Your House Plants

To keep your cat from digging in indoor flower pots, place a cotton ball dipped in oil of cloves just below the soil line.

If your pet is eating your house plants, here's a great product to try. It's called Bitter Apple and is simply sprayed on the plant leaves. It won't hurt the plant or your pet. Its bitter taste will immediately stop the pet from chewing on the plants. Try your local pet store.

Keeping Fleas Out of Dog Houses

To deter fleas, sprinkle salt in the crevices of the dog house.

If Your Pet Meets the Wrong End of a Skunk . . .

If your pet meets the wrong end of a skunk, apply Massengill™ douche, mixed as directed on the box. Do this outside and do not rinse. To help avoid eyes, apply a little petroleum jelly around the eye area.

14

Baby, Oh Baby and Kid's Corner

Kids are life's reward and add great joy to our lives. They also test all of our patience and cleaning skills. If you have children, large or small, or you have grandchildren, you need to memorize this chapter, or at least know where this book is at all times!

Baby Shoes

To make baby shoes easy to polish, rub them with the cut side of a raw potato or some rubbing alcohol prior to polishing. After polishing, spray with hair spray to keep the polish from rubbing off so easily. Put a little clear nail polish on the areas that are always scuffed and the shoes won't wear as much in those areas.

Bath Helpers

Put small slivers of mild soap into the open end of a small sock and tie shut, or make a small slit in a small size sponge and insert soap. These won't slip out of small hands (or yours when washing the baby).

For a great safe way to bathe a toddler, put a plastic laundry basket with mesh openings in the tub and put the child in it. It's a safe answer to bathing in the tub. But remember: Never leave a child alone in the bathtub.

Diaper Pins

If you are using cloth diapers, you know the misery of a dull diaper pin. To keep pins safely in one place where you can easily grab them and make them slide through fabric easily, store them stuck into a bar of soap.

Meal Mess Helper

To avoid those messy spills under baby's high chair, put a plastic tablecloth under it at mealtime. Cleanup will be a breeze and you can even put the tablecloth in the washing machine with an old towel, detergent and warm water. Hang to dry. This is a great tip when your toddler eats in Grandma's dining room!

Cleaning Stuffed Animals

Dust heavily with baking soda or cornstarch and work in well with your fingers. Roll the toys in towels or place in a plastic bag and leave overnight. The next day use a clean brush to brush the toys thoroughly after removing from the bag. Doing this outdoors saves cleanup.

Rattles and Teethers

A great place to wash these is in the dishwasher. Tie them in the top basket and wash with the dishes.

Formula Stains

On white clothes, apply undiluted lemon juice and lay the garment in the sun.

On colored clothes, make a paste of unseasoned meat tenderizer and cool water or an enzyme product from the laundry section at the grocery store. Apply and let sit for at least 30 minutes prior to laundering. Rubbing with a bar of wet Fels-Naptha Soap® will also help.

Cleaning Training Pants

To keep training pants white and odor-free, soak in a solution of 2 tablespoons of borax (available in the laundry section at the grocery store) and 1 gallon of hot water. Soak 1 hour prior to laundering.

To Remove Gum or Silly Putty™ from Hair

Rub cold cream or petroleum jelly into the gum. Use a dry Turkish towel-type rag to pull down on the hair strands and petroleum jelly. Work until all is out, then double shampoo.

That old reliable peanut butter also works great. Massage the gum and peanut butter together between your fingers until the gum is loosened and can be removed. Freeze the area with ice cubes in a plastic bag and then pick out the gum.

Crayon on Walls

Spray with WD-40™ lubricant. Wipe off with a paper towel. Wash with hot water and liquid dishwashing detergent, working in a circular motion. Rinse well.

Crayon on Fabric

Place the stained surface down on a pad of paper towels and spray with WD-40™, let stand a few minutes, turn over and spray the other side.

Again, let sit a few minutes. Apply dishwashing detergent and work into the stained area, replacing the toweling as it absorbs the stain. Wash in the hottest water for the fabric you are working with, using your regular laundry detergent and all-fabric bleach.

Watercolor Paint on Fabric

Brush and rinse as much of the watercolor from the surface as possible. Apply a soft-scrubbing product with a damp sponge and rub in a circular motion, working toward the center of the spot. Rinse and dry. If any stain remains, apply nail polish remover to a cotton ball, blot the stain and rinse. Repeat as needed.

Watercolor Paint on Carpet

Apply rubbing alcohol with a sponge, blotting the stained area lightly. Turn the sponge as the stain is absorbed. Repeat until no more stain is being removed. Most of the remaining stain can be removed with a damp sponge and soft-scrubbing product. Rinse carpet well.

Marker Marks on Appliances, Wood or Hard Plastic

Wipe all stains with a damp sponge. If any stain remains, apply a soft-scrubbing product with a damp sponge, working in a circular motion, and rinse. If the stain remains, saturate a cotton ball with nail polish remover, blot the remaining stain and rinse well. This works on paneling, painted wood, tile and no-wax vinyl floors.

Marker on Carpet

Dampen a sponge with rubbing alcohol and use a blotting motion to absorb the marker, changing the sponge as needed. Apply a good carpet spotter, such as Spot Shot Carpet Stain Remover®, as directed on the can.

Marker on Clothing

Rinse the stain from the fabric with cold water until no more color is being removed. Place the fabric on paper towels and saturate with rubbing alcohol, using a cotton ball or small cloth to blot the stain. Replace the paper towels as often as needed to prevent re-staining the fabric. Treat the stain with a lather from a bar of Fels-Naptha Soap® and launder as usual.

Chalk on Hard Surfaces

For colored or white chalk on masonry, painted surfaces, vinyl flooring, tile, plastic and glass, brush and rinse as much of the chalk from the surface as possible. Remove the remaining stain with a damp sponge or cloth dipped in a soft-scrubbing product. Rinse surface well.

Chalk on Carpet

Vacuum the area well, using the attachment hose to concentrate the suction over the chalk. If stain remains, use a good carpet-spotting product.

Colored Chalk on Fabric

Place the stained area on a pad of paper towels and blot the spot with rubbing alcohol. Work in a lather of Fels-Naptha Soap® and launder as usual.

Glue on Carpet and Fabric

For water-based glue such as Elmer's™ School Glue, fold a paper towel to overlap the glue spot and saturate to almost dripping with warm water. Place this on the glue spot and leave on for about 45 minutes to an hour to allow the glue to soften. Rub the glue spot with a wet rag in a circular motion to remove all the glue you can. Repeat this procedure until glue is removed. Follow with a good carpet spotter.

Silly Putty™ Clay and Similar Products on Carpet and Fabric

Scrape off what you can with the dull edge of a knife. Spray with WD-40™ lubricant and let stand about 10-15 minutes. Scrape again. Respray as required, wiping up the stain with an old rag. Once you have removed the residue of the product, apply rubbing alcohol to the stain and blot, blot, blot. Reapply as necessary.

To remove from hard surfaces, spray with WD-40™ lubricant and wipe with a paper towel or old rag. Wipe any remaining stain with a cloth saturated with rubbing alcohol. Wash with a solution of dishwashing liquid and hot water, working in a circular motion. Rinse well.

Writing on Plastic Toys and Doll Faces

Ink and marker are very difficult to remove from plastic surfaces. Try applying a cotton ball saturated with rubbing alcohol. Let sit for 15 minutes and then rub. Sometimes using the pressure of a cotton swab dipped in alcohol helps. You can also try rubbing with a little cuticle remover on a soft cloth. Apply the cuticle remover, wait 10 minutes and then rub gently with the cloth.

⑮
The Nose Knows—
Odor Control

One thing I have found is that most people associate clean with what they smell. We want everything to smell clean. Here are some ideas that will perk your nose right up.

Product Corner

For those of you looking for a foolproof product you can purchase to use in eliminating all odors with success, I highly recommend the product ODORZOUT®.

This is a 100 percent natural product that stops many odors almost on contact—odors such as urine, mold, mildew, smoke, foot odor, skunk, paint and virtually every odor you can smell. It is made of blended natural zeolite minerals, contains no perfumes and is 100 percent safe for use around children or pets. You can even use it in the cat litterbox. In my testing, I have found no odor it didn't work on. Call 800-88STINK for more information or ordering, or visit the website: www.88stink.com.

Burned Food

Boil a few slices of lemon in a saucepan to clear the air of the smell of burned food.

Fried Food

This works on any fried food odor, but the next time you fry fish, be sure to try it. Place a small bowl of white vinegar next to the stove when you fry foods. The odor seems to disappear.

Refrigerators

To deodorize refrigerators, leave a bowl filled with clean clay cat litter or charcoal on the shelf to absorb odors. This is particularly helpful in refrigerators that are going to be shut off or moved. Make sure you leave the door partially open at all times to allow air circulation, and put some litter or charcoal in an old nylon stocking and tie the top shut. Lay this in the refrigerator and it will control odors. For strong odors, nothing works better than dry, fresh coffee grounds. Put them in a bowl and leave in the refrigerator until odor disappears. This can be used in conjunction with the cat litter or charcoal very effectively.

Cars

If you smoke in the car, put a layer of baking soda in the bottom of the ashtray to absorb smoke odor. Empty it frequently. Dryer fabric softener sheets placed under the seats also help to keep the smoke smell under control. For musty smells, put cat litter in a nylon stocking, tie the top shut and place several under the seats or in the trunk.

Wood Trunks, Dressers and Chests

Many times old wood trunks and dressers will have a musty mildew or old odor. To eliminate this take a slice of white bread (yes, it has to be white), put it in a bowl and cover with white vinegar. Leave enclosed in the trunk or drawers for 24 hours. If odor remains, repeat the process. If mildew odor persists in dresser drawers, shellac or varnish the inside of them and odor will be sealed in and eliminated.

Home Odors

Wintergreen oil is a wonderful deodorant. Purchase some at a health food store and put a few drops on cotton balls and stash in plants, decorative pieces, etc., around the house.

Make Your Own Air Freshener

In a gallon jug combine 1 cup baking soda, ¼ cup clear ammonia and 1 tablespoon scent (use your imagination— any scented oils or extracts work). Slowly add 16 cups of warm water, label and store. To use, pour well-shaken solution into a spray container and mist air as needed.

16

Hot Tips for Irons and Ironing Boards

Cleaning an Iron That Does Not Have a Nonstick Surface

Heat the iron to the hot, nonsteam setting. Run it over table salt sprinkled on a brown paper grocery bag.

You can also use non-gel toothpaste. Apply it to a damp cloth and rub over the soleplate on a cool iron until starch buildup and ironing residue are removed. Rinse well.

For terrible buildup, burned-on fabric or starch, take the iron outside and cover all parts of the iron except soleplate with paper. Spray oven cleaner directly onto the soleplate of a cool iron. Wait several minutes and then rinse off well with cool water and an old rag or sponge.

With a Nonstick Surface

Use laundry pre-spotter. Rub on and rinse off well.

After Cleaning

After cleaning your iron with any of these methods, remember to rinse it well and then fill with water, heat on the heavy steam setting and iron over old fabric prior to using on clothes. This will remove any residue remaining in the vent holes.

Cleaning the Vent Holes

Many times the vent holes in the bottom of the iron will become clogged. Take a pipe cleaner and clean out each hole individually.

Always empty steam irons after each use to prevent clogging.

Cleaning the Internal Parts

Fill the steam iron with equal portions of water and white vinegar. Let it steam for several minutes. Disconnect the iron and let it sit for one hour. Empty and rinse with clear water using the same process. Be sure to iron over old fabric prior to ironing clothes.

Keeping Ironing Board Covers Clean

To make covers last longer and stay clean longer, spray them with spray starch once the cover is on the board and iron the starch in well.

Energy-Efficient Ironing

Put aluminum foil under the ironing board cover when you put it on the board. It will reflect heat onto the garments as you iron and cut ironing time.

⑰ Taking Charge of Electronic Equipment

Telephones

To clean and disinfect telephone receivers, apply Listerine™ mouthwash with a soft cotton pad or rag. Do not rinse off. This is great advice for offices during cold and flu season.

Television Screens

Denatured alcohol (available at hardware stores) makes a great cleaner for many pieces of electronic equipment. To clean the TV screen, turn off the power to the TV. Apply alcohol to a rag or paper towel and wipe the screen thoroughly, then buff.

Stop Dust from Settling

Apply antistatic product to a rag and wipe the screen and cabinet, or mix 1 part liquid fabric softener to 4 parts water and apply with a soft cloth and buff.

Radios

These need to be dusted often. Clean them occasionally with denatured alcohol applied with a cotton ball. Do not use alcohol on wood.

Cameras

Cameras should always be stored in their cases when not in use. This prevents them from becoming dusty. Except for wiping off the outside of the lens with a cotton ball and a little alcohol, leave cleaning to the professionals.

Videocassette Recorders

These need to be kept free of dust to stay in good working order. It is best to cover them with a plastic cover when not in use. If the room is damp, keep silica packets (available from florists or many times found in new leather shoes or purses) on top of the VCR (keep these packets away from children). Clean the VCR occasionally using a cleaning tape to ensure good-quality pictures on playback. Store videotapes in cardboard or plastic cases to keep them clean and in good condition for playback or recording.

Answering Machines

These need to be dusted with a lambswool duster, particularly inside the machine. You can use an aerosol cleaner, but make sure that the machine is dry before you replace the cassette.

Fax Machines

These also need to be kept dusted and occasionally wiped with denatured alcohol.

Compact Discs

To keep your compact discs clean, mix 2 tablespoons of baking soda and 1 pint of water in a spray bottle. Shake well to mix and spray on the disc, wiping with a soft cloth. Do not wipe in a circular motion; wipe from the center hole in the disc out to the outside edge.

Computers

To avoid costly problems with computers, it is important that they be kept dust-free. Dust between the keys of your keyboard with a cotton swab, or vacuum with the duster-brush on your vacuum or with a special computer vacuum that helps you get between the keys.

Mix 1 part water and 1 part alcohol and apply to the keys

with a cotton swab. Don't overwet. Undiluted denatured alcohol may also be used in the same manner.

Dust the screen and spray with an antistatic product.

Make sure that computers are situated out of direct sunlight, which can cause overheating. Sunlight also makes it difficult for the user to see the computer screen clearly.

A Special Reminder

Never clean any electronic equipment without unplugging it first!

18

The Care and Hanging of Pictures and Paintings

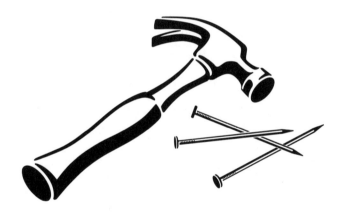

Pictures and paintings are part of the personal touches that make a house a home. Here are some ideas for hanging and cleaning pictures and oil and acrylic paintings.

Finding the Stud the Easy Way

When you are ready to hang a picture, especially a heavy one, it is a good idea to find a stud to hang it from. Take an electric razor and run it across the wall. You will notice a distinct difference in the sound of the razor going over a hollow wall and the sound when it hits a stud. Use this whenever you need to find the stud to hang anything around the house.

Keeping Cockeyed Pictures Straight

Wind some adhesive tape around the center of the picture wire. The wire will be less likely to slip on the hanger.

Place masking tape on the back four corners of your picture and press against the wall. Wrap masking tape, sticky side out, around the middle of a round toothpick and place a few near the bottom, backside of the frame.

Preventing Experimental Holes

Cut a paper pattern of each picture or mirror that you plan to hang and pin to the wall. After you've found the correct positions for the hangers, perforate the paper with a sharp pencil to mark the wall.

When you want to avoid nail holes in the walls, hang pictures with a sewing machine needle. They hold up to 30 pounds and leave almost no marks on the wall.

Staining Unfinished Picture Frames

Stain them beautifully with ordinary liquid shoe polish. Apply one coat and let dry. Follow with another coat, then wax with a good paste wax. Brown shoe polish gives the wood a walnut glow and oxblood emulates a mahogany or cherry color. Tan polish will look like a light maple. This hides scratches, too.

Cleaning Glass-Covered Pictures

Never spray any cleaner directly on the glass; it may seep under and onto the picture. Spray a paper towel with window cleaner, wipe and polish with a dry towel.

Polish glass with a used fabric softener sheet to shine and deter dust.

Cleaning Oil and Acrylic Paintings

Give them an occasional dusting with a clean, lint-free cloth or a soft brush. Spot-clean if necessary with a barely damp rag or piece of white bread. If the painting is worth a lot of money or has sentimental value, take it to a professional. Even a soft dust cloth can snag and cause a chip.

Gilt Picture Frames

Remove stains from gilt picture frames by rubbing gently with a cloth moistened in milk.

Photo Emergency

If you have a picture that is stuck to the glass, immerse the glass and the photo in a pan of room-temperature water and keep testing until the photo pulls free. Don't try to rush it! Let the photo air-dry. Since most photo prints get a water bath during processing, there shouldn't be any damage, though this is not a 100 percent guarantee.

19
Paint by Numbers

One of the questions men ask me most frequently is how to get through the job of painting quickly and make it easier. Actually, there are things you can do to make the job go much more smoothly.

Short-term Storage

If you need to store a paintbrush or roller in the middle of a project or between coats of paint, place it in a tightly sealed plastic bag and place in the freezer. The brush or roller will not dry out for a day or two and no cleanup is needed until you have completed the project.

Protect Hardware

When painting woodwork, cover door knobs, locks and other hardware with a generous coat of petroleum jelly. If the paint splashes where it shouldn't, it can easily be wiped up.

Splatter Removal

For easy removal of paint splatters on window panes, use a round typewriter eraser with a brush on the end—it's safer than a razor and easy, too!

Painting Screws

To make painting screws from hardware easier, stick them in a piece of foam packing material. The screw heads will all be facing up, ready to be sprayed or painted in one coat.

Cleaning Hands

Use vegetable oil to clean oil-based paints off hands. The oil is safer than paint thinner, has no fumes and is mild to the skin. After using the oil, wash well with soap.

Preventing White Paint from Yellowing

To stop white paint from yellowing with age, put several drops of black paint in for every quart of white paint. Mix very well.

Keep Cans Clean

Cover the rim of the paint can with masking tape if you are going to pour paint from the can. When you are done, remove the tape to clean the top.

Drip Realignment

If you are painting from the can, punch two or three nail holes in the small groove in the top rim of your paint can. As you wipe the paint from your brush on the rim, the paint will drip back into the can instead of collecting in the groove and spilling over and down the sides of the can.

Clean Brushes in a Second

To make a paintbrush easier to clean, wrap masking tape around the metal ferrule and about ½ inch over the bristles. Rather than drying on the bristles, paint will collect on the masking tape. To clean, remove the tape and clean the paint that remains on the brush.

Garbage Garment

Wear a garbage bag as a cover-all when painting overhead. Cut a hole for head and arms. You can cover your head with an old shower cap. No more paint splatters on clothes and hair!

Easier-Opening Cans

When sealing the lid on a paint can, wipe a thin layer of petroleum jelly around the rim. This will allow the can to open easily the next time.

Record-Keeping

Before you store leftover paint, list the rooms you have painted with it on the can. Touch-ups are easier if you don't have to try to figure out which can of paint you used for what.

Paint-Catching Wristband

If you paint like I do and have runs of paint going down your arms every time you paint over your head, wrap an old washcloth around your wrist, secure with a rubber band and remove and throw away when you are done painting.

Dry Brushes Completely

If you soak your brush between painting sessions, be sure to drain out all of the liquid or you will have a dripping mess when you start painting again. One good way to do this is to stand the brush straight up in an empty can for a few min-

utes to let the fluid drip out or suspend it from a stick laid across the top of an empty can that is taller than the brush. To be absolutely sure that the brush is dry, take an old rag, wrap it around the brush and squeeze the bristles from the top downward over the can.

Where to Start

Start painting at the top of the wall and work your way down. That way, if paint drips down it can be smoothed out as you go.

When to Start

No need to get up early to paint outside. You don't want to start painting until after the morning dew has evaporated. But, remember, never paint in the direct sunlight.

⓴ The Grill Drill

L et's talk about ways to make cooking on the grill easier and more fun.

Prevent Sticking

Before you light the barbecue, spray the grill rack with non-stick cooking spray. This works great on gas or charcoal grills. Apply a liberal coat and food won't stick, making cooking and cleanup a lot easier.

Cleaning the Grill

To clean the grill surface when it is heavily caked with baked-on food, follow this procedure. Simply wrap the rack in a piece of heavy-duty aluminum foil, dull side facing out. Heat the barbecue to high heat and place the rack over the coals or flame for approximately 10 to 12 minutes. When you remove the foil after it has cooled, all the burned-on grease and food drippings will fall off and your rack will be spotless and ready to grill again.

Immediately After Cooking

Make a ball of aluminum foil and "scrub" the warm grill rack surface with it, taking care not to burn your fingers.

The Bathtub Method and a Less-Messy Version

Many people recommend putting the grill rack in the bathtub filled with hot water, detergent and ammonia. I find this a particularly messy way to do it because you have to clean the tub when you're done. If you do use this method, be sure to lay old rags or a garbage bag in the tub to prevent scratching the tub surface with the grill rack.

I suggest you try this method instead. Lay some paper towels moistened with undiluted ammonia on both sides of the rack. Put it in an appropriate-size plastic bag and seal.

Leave it overnight and the next day open the bag, away from your face—it stinks. Wipe down with the paper towels in the bag, wash with soapy water and rinse.

Keeping Pan Bottoms Clean

Before setting a pan on the grill rack to warm barbecue sauce or cook additional foods, rub the pan bottom with bar soap and it will be easier to clean the soot off when you are done.

Cleaning Permanent Briquettes

Flip the briquettes occasionally and ignite the grill with the cover closed. Allow it to burn at a high setting for about 15 minutes.

Grease Splatters

For cement or wood patios, keep a container of salt nearby when barbecuing. Should grease spatter or drip, immediately cover with salt. Sweep up and reapply until grease is absorbed. Scrub with dishwashing liquid and rinse.

Keeping the Outside of the Grill Clean

This is such a fast, easy way to clean the outside of the grill. It works well on charcoal and gas grills and will make them look almost like new. Take some Go-Jo Waterless Hand Cleaner® (available at grocery stores, hardware stores and home centers) and rub it on the outside of a cool grill with an old rag or paper towel. Work it into the metal well, paying special attention to any grease or barbecue sauce spots. Do not rinse; instead, take paper towels and buff the grill surface and watch as the dirt is replaced by a great shine.

Keeping the Glass Grill Window Clean

Many gas grills have glass windows in them. Of course, once you use the grill a few times you can no longer see through the window! To clean this, spray the inside of the glass with oven cleaner. Wait a few minutes and then scrub and rinse well. On the outside of the glass use Go-Jo Waterless Hand Cleaner® and buff well.

21
Everything Under the Sun for Patio Furniture

No matter what part of the country you live in, at some time you have to clean the outdoor furniture. Follow this advice to make the job go faster.

Furniture Cushions

There are several ways to clean outdoor furniture cushions. You can use Spot Shot Upholstery Stain Remover® or Spot Shot Instant Carpet Stain Remover®. Follow the directions on the can. Or, mix your own solution. In a spray bottle combine 1 teaspoon of dishwashing liquid and 1 teaspoon of borax per quart of warm water. Spray this on the cushion on both sides and let it sit for about 15 minutes. Then take out the hose and, using a strong spray, rinse the solution and the dirt off the cushions. Put them back on the chairs and set them out of the direct sun to dry. Once they have dried to just damp, apply a good coating of Scotchgard™ Fabric Protector® (available at grocery stores and home centers) to protect the cushions and make cleaning easier the next time. Vacuum the cushions as needed to remove dust between cleanings.

Aluminum

Although it doesn't rust, aluminum can become dull and pitted when left outdoors. To clean and restore the shine, scrub the frames with a plastic scrubber soaked in detergent or a soap-filled steel wool pad, then rinse and dry.

Aluminum with Baked-Enamel Finish

Use a sponge soaked in detergent and wash well, rinse and dry. To protect, apply a coat of good-quality car wax. This will make cleaning easier and maintain the shine. It can be used on tables with a baked-enamel finish, too.

Canvas

Soiled canvas seats and chair backs are usually machine washable, but be sure to put them back on the furniture when they are still damp to maintain their shape. To clean canvas that you cannot put in the washing machine, such as large seats, backs or awnings, run a scrub brush back and forth across a bar of Fels-Naptha Soap®. Rub this back and forth across the canvas and then rinse well. This will even remove bird droppings and, many times, the staining, too.

Plastic

Wash with good all-purpose cleaner and water, then rinse with water and dry. An alternative for white furniture is automatic dishwasher detergent and warm water (1 gallon warm water to 3 tablespoons automatic dishwasher detergent). Wash and let solution sit on the furniture for 15 minutes or so and then rinse and dry.

Maintaining Shine

To maintain the shine on plastic, resin and metal furniture, apply a good-quality paste car wax just as you would when waxing a car.

22
All Hands on Decks

Acertain amount of routine maintenance is required to keep your backyard deck structurally sound, safe and looking its best.

Though other types of lumber may have been used, chances are that your deck is built of cedar, redwood or pressure-treated yellow pine. These are the most commonly used materials for decks because they are resistant to rot and insect damage. When exposed to the elements for extended periods of time, any wood will show signs of weathering. Even if the deck was originally treated with stain or a preservative, this treatment eventually needs to be renewed.

Inspect and Protect

The first thing you need to do once the weather turns nice is inspect the deck surfaces for any splintering, which you will need to sand. Pay special attention to the railing.

You'll find many stains and sealers designed for decks. Several manufacturers now offer products called deck brighteners, which actually bleach the surface to remove stains and weathering on wood surfaces. Apply these products carefully, following the instructions. Usually you will brush the product on with a stiff bristle brush, and rinse off thoroughly prior to applying any finish coating.

Sealers protect the deck from moisture and are available in clear or tinted varieties to act as a stain. Sealers require periodic renewal to maintain protection.

Now go over the actual decking to be sure it is tight and in place, fixing whatever is required. Finally, if no repair or staining is needed, follow some of these suggestions to give the deck a good cleaning.

If there are leaves and other debris on the deck, either sweep or use a blower to remove it.

Hose Off the Deck

With a garden hose and a strong—and preferably long-handled—brush, use the strongest spray setting on the nozzle to break up dirt on the surface. Follow this with the brush to loosen any stubborn soil. This works especially well with two people, who can take turns hosing and scrubbing.

Kill Mildew

Check the condition of the wood. Green or black areas indicate mold and mildew. To remove mold and mildew from the wood you will need either a commercial deck-cleaning product (which may be purchased at your local home center) or you can prepare your own using a mixture of 1 cup trisodium phosphate (available at janitorial supply stores and home centers), 1 gallon of oxygen-type bleach (safer to use than chlorine bleach) and 1 gallon of hot water. The bleach will kill the mildew and the TSP will thoroughly clean the wood surface. You can apply this with a garden sprayer or mop it on.

First wet down the deck with the hose and then apply the cleaning solution. Spread the solution evenly and scrub with the brush you used earlier. Let the solution sit for about 15 minutes and then hose off. Repeat the wetting, bleaching and rinsing process as necessary until the entire deck is clean. Make sure you do stairs, handrails and any other deck parts.

After you have done the entire deck, I recommend that you hose down the grass and any plants surrounding it to remove any solution that has dripped on them. No damage should be done to plants, but rinsing is a good precaution. If you have used a garden sprayer, be sure to wash it out well and rinse the brush before storing.

Quick Cleaning

To give the deck a quick cleaning during the use season, mix up a gallon of hot water and ¼ cup of any good-quality household cleaner, or 1 gallon of hot water, 1 tablespoon of dishwashing liquid and ¼ cup of borax. Mop the deck down with one of these solutions and rinse well. Again, be sure to rinse plants and grass down.

Removing Sap from an Unfinished Wood Deck

Tree sap can be a problem on wood decks. To remove it, apply mineral spirits with an old rag, rub and wash off with dishwashing liquid and water (1 teaspoon of dishwashing liquid to 1 quart of hot water). Rinse well.

23

Concrete Solutions for Cleaning Cement Driveways and Patios

One question everyone asks is how to clean cement driveways, garage floors and patios. The best time to clean cement is when the temperature is between 50 and 75 degrees and the direct sun is not shining on it. Take this into consideration when using the cleaning methods in this chapter.

Grab the Dust on Cement

To make quick work of sweeping a cement garage floor or patio, pick up some sweeping compound at either a janitorial supply store, hardware store or home center. The sweeping compound will "grab" the dust instead of spreading it in the air as you sweep. When you're done, just sweep it into a dust pan and throw out.

Kitty Litter™— a Garage Floor's Best Friend

Cat box litter, either regular clay or clumping, is wonderful for absorbing liquid spills, especially oil of any kind. Simply pour it on the spot and then—the secret to success—grind it into the spot with your foot. Leave it and allow it to absorb all of the oil that it can. Then sweep up. Repeat the process if necessary.

Old Stains on Cement

Apply a spray-and-wash product and leave it on for 5-10 minutes. Sprinkle with laundry detergent, scrub with a stiff brush or broom and then rinse.

Another good method is to make a paste of hot water and automatic dishwasher detergent. Scrub it into the spot and let it soak for at least one hour or overnight. Add additional water and scrub, then rinse well.

Removing the Toughest Stains

Use oven cleaner to remove the toughest spots. Spray it on, keeping your face well back. Let it stand for 15 minutes and then scrub with a stiff brush or broom and hose off. Repeat if necessary. Do not allow children or pets in the area when using this method. Rinse cement and brush with plenty of water. Do not combine other cleaning products with the oven cleaner until it is rinsed well with water.

Removing Rust from Concrete

Wet the concrete and sprinkle with lemon Kool-Aid™. Cover with plastic and soak for 15 minutes. Remove plastic, scrub with a brush and rinse well.

Another method that may work for you is applying ZUD Heavy Duty Cleanser®. This can be purchased at the store in the cleanser section. Make a paste with warm water and work in well with a brush. Let soak for 30 minutes and then scrub with additional hot water and rinse well.

If the rust stain is really bad, you will have to use a solution of 10 parts water to 1 part muriatic acid. Let this sit 2-3 hours and then scrub with a stiff (nonmetallic) brush. Use extreme caution if you use this method. Wear goggles, gloves and old clothes, and rinse, rinse, rinse! Keep children and pets away from the area while using the acid.

㉔
At the Carwash

Auto Quick Tips

Stain guard

Before long trips, spray the front of your car, where the bugs collect, with nonstick cooking spray. This will stop bugs from sticking, and bugs and dirt can be easily washed off.

Cleaning the windshield

Clean your windshield with baking soda and water prior to washing the car. White vinegar added to a wet, lint-free rag will remove grease film and give you a streak-free shine.

Bug scraper

Save the plastic net bags from produce such as onions to scrub the window when it is spattered with bugs. Keep a couple in the car to use at the gas station when washing your windows and then throw them away. Great to have on hand when you're traveling.

Removing tar

Saturate tar spots with linseed oil. Let soak and then rub with an old rag or paper towel moistened with the oil.

Removing bumper stickers

Use a blow-dryer to heat the sticker, then use a flat edge, such as an old credit card, and start peeling. Continue to heat and peel. Remove residue with nail polish remover.

Chrome

If you have dirty chrome on your car, simply dampen a piece of aluminum foil and rub. This is a great way to remove rust, too.

Battery corrosion stopper

Scrub the battery terminals and the holder with ½ cup of baking soda combined with 2 cups warm water. When dry, apply petroleum jelly to the area.

Preventing doors from freezing

Spray the rubber gaskets around the door and trunk with nonstick cooking spray. This will keep water out and also keep the gaskets supple. Remember this trick if you plan on having the car washed in cold weather.

Making windshield washer solvent

This can be used in the windshield washer container in your car—winter or summer. It will not freeze and is a great cleaner. Combine 1 quart rubbing alcohol, 1 cup water and 2 tablespoons of liquid dishwashing detergent or laundry detergent. This should not freeze even at 30 degrees below zero.

Removing salt residue from carpet

Combine a 50-50 solution of white vinegar and water. Apply to carpet and blot. Reapply as necessary.

General interior cleaning

For spots on carpet and upholstery, count on a good carpet spotter such as Spot Shot Instant Carpet Stain Remover®. Use as directed on the can.

For leather upholstery

Wet a soft cloth with warm water and rub it across a wet bar of Dove Moisturizing Soap® several times. Wash the seats thoroughly, rinsing out the cloth and reapplying the soap as it becomes soiled. Do not rinse; instead, dry with a soft cloth.

Professional Interior Cleaning

To really give your car a complete cleaning, rent an extraction machine at the hardware store or home center and clean upholstered seats and carpet thoroughly. Be sure to leave the windows down to allow the interior to dry completely.

㉕
Do Away with Window Pains

To achieve professional results you need to use the same tools the professionals use. You can find all of these things at either a janitorial supply store (look in the yellow pages) or a hardware store.

Use the Right Tools

Squeegee

A good squeegee is an absolute must. Don't be fooled into thinking that a cheap plastic squeegee or a car windshield squeegee will do the job—they won't! The best size to start with is a 12- or 14-inch squeegee. This will work well on most windows, and once you have mastered this size you can move up to an 18-inch for large-paned windows and down to a 6-inch for small French panes.

Scrubber

A good scrubber is a plus. This tool looks like a squeegee wearing a fluffy coat. It is used to wet and clean the window prior to using the squeegee. If you do not want to invest in this, be sure you buy a good natural sponge.

Rag or Chamois

Use a dry rag or chamois for drying the squeegee rubber (blade) and the edges of the glass.

Scraper

Use a window scraper for removing paint, concrete and other stubborn debris. If you don't purchase this you can use a good medium- to fine-grade steel wool pad. If you use this be sure the pad and the window are soapy wet. Never use one of those scrub pads that you use on dishes; this will scratch the glass. Never use steel wool on tinted glass.

Extension Pole

If you have difficult, high, hard-to-reach windows, you might consider an extension pole made for a squeegee. This will enable you to stand on the ground and reach the high windows without a ladder.

Bucket and TSP

A bucket of water and TSP, trisodium phosphate, or dishwashing detergent (2 or 3 squirts to a bucket) added after you have filled the bucket with water.

Let's Get Started

Fill your bucket with warm water and add the TSP or dishwashing liquid.

Be sure you have all the necessary equipment laid out and ready for use.

Follow the steps listed below, in order. You'll be cleaning like a pro in no time!

Dip your scrubber or sponge into the cleaning solution and wash the window thoroughly, using a very wet steel wool pad to remove any stubborn spots, such as bug stains. You do not have to press too hard on the steel wool pad. Rewet the window so you will have time to squeegee the window before it dries. Try not to clean in the direct sunlight, as it will cause streaking and spotting.

Tilt the squeegee at an angle so that 2 inches of rubber blade touches the glass. Start at the top corner and draw the squeegee along the top edge of the window.

Wipe the squeegee blade on a sponge, start on the dry surface close to the frame and draw the squeegee down to within about 3 inches of the bottom of the glass.

Repeat this stroke until you have squeegeed all of the glass. Be sure you overlap each stroke and wipe the squeegee blade after each stroke.

Soak up excess water with a well-rinsed sponge.

Do the same thing you did in step two at the top of the glass, this time working at the bottom of the glass.

Have your rag or chamois handy to wipe the window edges if needed. If you see a streak on the window, let it dry, then use poly/cotton rag, such as an old T-shirt, to polish it out.

Spray-and-Wipe Cleaning Solutions

If you prefer to wash your windows the spray-and-wipe way, here are a couple of good cleaning solutions.

Polishing Glass or Removing Screen and Bug Stains

Make a thin paste of baking soda and water, rub onto glass, rinse well and dry with a soft cloth.

Easy Window Cleaner

Combine:

    2 quarts warm water
    ½ cup cornstarch

Apply to window with a sponge and buff dry with paper towels or soft, lint-free rags.

Tough-Job Window Cleaner

Combine:

    1 pint rubbing alcohol
    2 tablespoons clear ammonia
    2 tablespoons dishwashing liquid

Apply to the window using a nylon-covered sponge, rinse and buff dry. Great for hard-water spots.

Screen Savers

Most people just hose screens down to clean them. This just moves the dirt from one part of the screen to the other. Here's a better way. Just soap the screen with a sponge dipped in a pail of warm water containing 2 tablespoons of dishwashing liquid, ¼ cup of ammonia and 2 tablespoons of borax. Really suds up the screen. Now lay a rag on the ground and gently tap the screen on it. Most of the soapy water containing the dirt will come off this way. To finish, rinse the screen with the hose and stand to dry, or rag dry.

Bad News

Remember, no matter what you have heard about cleaning windows with newspaper, don't do it. It is a dirty, messy way and leaves newsprint all over white window trim and paint.

QUICK TIP ....
Use a dry blackboard eraser on a dry window or mirror after cleaning to banish any streaks you've left behind!

26
Flower Power

Making Fresh Flowers Last Longer

To make fresh flowers from your garden or floral arrangements from the florist last longer, use the following recipe. Remove any foliage below the waterline, trim the stem ends periodically and keep the solution fresh and your flowers will live longer.

Combine:

    1 quart of water

    2 tablespoons of lemon juice

    1 tablespoon sugar

    ½ teaspoon liquid bleach

Add the solution to the flower container and enjoy. If you have an arrangement from the florist, add this solution each time you add water.

If you don't have the above ingredients on hand, add 2 ounces of Listerine™ mouthwash per gallon of water.

To make cut flowers last longer without shedding, spray with hair spray. Hold the spray can about a foot away from the flowers and spray in an upward direction to prevent the flowers from drooping.

Cleaning Vases

To easily clean a flower vase, fill with warm water and add one or two denture-cleaning tablets, depending on the size of the vase. Let it soak at least an hour or overnight. Wash, rinse and dry well. If you don't have any denture-cleaning tablets, throw in a handful of dry rice and some white vinegar and shake, shake, shake. Let soak with vinegar and warm water if necessary. Wash and rinse the vase well.

Transporting Fresh Flowers

If you are taking fresh flowers from your garden as a gift, or to the office, fill a balloon with water, put the stems in and secure the neck of the balloon to the stems with a rubber band, twist tie or ribbon. Poking the stems through a paper doily will also hold the stems in place and make an attractive presentation. Your flowers will arrive fresh-looking at their destination with no spilled water to worry about!

The Dirt on Flower Pots

When planting flowers in a pot with a drainage hole in the bottom, line the bottom of the pot with enough coffee filters to cover it. Add a few pebbles and then add the soil. When you water the plant the dirt won't run out the bottom.

Flower Filler

When planting shallow-rooted flowers in a large pot, line the bottom with coffee filters and pebbles, fill the pot ⅓ full of packing peanuts and then fill with soil. The pot will be much lighter to move and you won't require as much soil to fill the pot.

Healthful Water

When you boil eggs, save the water to water your plants. It is full of minerals.

Cold coffee or tea combined with water provides an acidic drink for your plants. (Be sure it doesn't run out on the carpet.)

Water from an aquarium provides excellent fertilizer for plants.

Club soda that has lost its fizz is good for plants.

Going on vacation? Stand plants in the sink or bathtub, depending on the number you have. Be sure they are in pots with a hole in the bottom. Add a few inches of water to the tub and plants will be automatically watered while you are gone. To preserve the tub finish, lay an old towel in the bottom to set plants on.

Unbugged

If bugs are a problem on indoor plants, spray the soil with insect spray and immediately cover the plant with a plastic bag. Leave in place for a couple of days and then uncover.

Let Them Shine

To shine indoor plant leaves, wipe gently with glycerin. Another great way to add shine is by wiping leaves with a mixture of half milk and half water. Do not use oil on plant leaves, as it attracts dust and dirt.

Window Boxes and Patio Flower Pots

These are easy to keep clean. After you plant the flowers in the pots, put a layer of gravel or marbles on top. When you water or it rains, the dirt won't splash all over the plants, pots, patio or porch.

Hanging Plants

To water hanging plants with ease and without the mess of water running all over, use ice cubes. The cubes melt slowly and won't allow water to run out onto the floor or patio.

Weed Prevention

To kill weeds growing in sidewalk cracks, pour boiling salt water on them. Use a mixture of ¼ cup salt to 2 quarts water.

To prevent the weeds from growing in the cracks, sprinkle salt into the cracks.

Cleaning Artificial Flowers

To really clean and remove soil from artificial flowers, dried silk or polyester, place them in a bag with table salt. Add salt in proportion to the size of the flowers. Close the bag and shake the flowers in the salt for several minutes, or longer if the flowers are heavily soiled. Shake gently to remove the salt. The salt won't look dirty when you are done, but if you run water into it, you will be surprised how much dirt is removed from the flowers.

You can also place silk flowers in a pillowcase, tie a knot in it and put it in the clothes dryer on "air fluff" or "air only" for about 15 to 20 minutes.

Spray polyester flowers with acrylic spray from the craft store and they will resist soiling. If they get very dusty, wash under a mild stream of running water, shake and stand up to dry.

27
Bug Out— User-Friendly Pest Control

Are the bugs bugging you? Are the pests pestering you? You can control bugs without chemicals, the safe, environmentally friendly way. When planting flowers or controlling insects inside the house, keep this guide handy.

Insect Repellent

When using insect sprays, especially those containing DEET, try spraying clothes instead of skin—it's much safer, especially for children.

Or Try Vinegar

A wonderful substitute for insect repellent is white vinegar. Apply it to the skin with a cotton ball, applying liberally. Bugs hate the way you taste and the smell of the vinegar disappears once it dries. Great for kids!

Aphids

Mix nonfat dry milk with water according to the directions on the box, then put in a spray bottle and apply it to the leaves of your plants. As the milk dries, the aphids get stuck in the milky residue and die. You can rinse the plants from time to time with the hose. This will not harm your plants and offers an inexpensive solution to a big problem.

Aphids and Spiders

Wash off the plant with a mild solution of dishwashing liquid and water. Try a ratio of ½ teaspoon dishwashing liquid to 1 quart water. Flush leaves, including undersides, with the solution. Do not rinse off.

Aphids and Whiteflies

These bugs are attracted to bright yellow and can be trapped by placing a yellow board or other yellow objects such as yellow poster board, oleo lids, or sticks painted yellow, coated with heavy motor oil, petroleum jelly or Tack Trap® near susceptible plants. Recoat when the traps dry out.

Aphids on Roses

Use 1½ teaspoons of baking soda per pint of water and apply every seven days. This method is user-, earth- and child-friendly.

Grasshoppers

To deter grasshoppers, plant basil around the flower bed borders. Grasshoppers will eat the basil and leave the plants alone.

Ants

For ants on the counter, wipe the counter down with undiluted white vinegar.

To prevent ants from coming in the house, or getting into cupboards, sprinkle dried mint or red pepper where they are entering the house and in the cupboards.

To get rid of anthills, pour 3 gallons of boiling water down them. This is best done when the ants are active and near the surface. Do not do this close to flowers or they will die, too.

Another way to kill ants is to mix a combination of 50 percent borax and 50 percent confectioner's sugar. Place this on cardboard or a piece of board near the ant hill. The ants are attracted by the sugar and carry the fatal borax/sugar combination back to the nest to feed the queen and other ants. Soon all are dead. A note of caution: Do not place this where children or pets may ingest this mixture. Borax is sold in the laundry aisle at the grocery store as a laundry additive, not as a pesticide.

Cockroaches

To keep cockroaches out of the cupboards, place some bay leaves on the shelves.

Kill cockroaches with a mixture of ⅓ borax, ⅓ cornmeal, ⅓ flour and a dash of powdered sugar. Sprinkle this in crevices under sinks and vanities where cockroaches love to hide. Remember, keep this away from children and animals.

You can also try this formula for cockroaches: Mix powdered boric acid with sugar and powdered nondairy creamer. I use a mixture of 50 percent boric acid to 25 percent each sugar and creamer. This is inexpensive and relatively safe, but it should be kept away from children and pets. Sprinkle the mixture in all the dark, warm places that cockroaches love— under sinks and stoves, behind refrigerators, in cabinets and closets, and so on. The roaches will walk through the powder and then clean themselves, much the way a cat preens. Once they ingest the powder they die.

28

Putting Your Best Foot Forward

hat article of clothing gets more wear and tear than our shoes? Many of us have a favorite pair of tennis shoes that we live in. When we come home we take them off after a hot day at work, and our family leaves the room making comments about a skunk smelling better. Now, there is a quick, easy answer to shoe odor. Taking good care of shoes will make them look better, of course, but it will also extend the life of the shoes, too.

Cleaning and Deodorizing Shoes

This method will work with any shoe. First, sprinkle some baking soda in the shoe, then place it in a plastic bag and freeze it for a night or two. Allow the shoe to come to room temperature (unless you want to cool your feet) and then shake out the baking soda and wear. It is a good idea to leave the baking soda in the shoe until the next wearing.

Stretching Shoes

Here's another freezer tip for the pair of shoes that pinches your toes. For each shoe use a heavy-duty zip closure bag, or double up two of them and put them in each shoe. Carefully pour water into the bags, until the toe area is full. Close the bags securely so the water doesn't seep out and wet the shoes. To help prevent the outside of the shoes from getting wet, put each shoe in a plastic bag. Place the shoes in the freezer for at least 24 hours. As the water freezes it expands, and as it does this the shoes will expand and stretch. You will need to allow the shoes to defrost enough to remove the bags of water when you remove them from the freezer.

Cleaning White Canvas Shoes

Apply a paste of automatic dishwashing detergent mixed with hot water to the shoes. Allow to soak at least 30 minutes, then scrub surface with a nail brush or toothbrush. Rinse well and allow to dry. Dry the shoes out of the direct sun. You can also put the shoes in the washing machine with several old white towels and launder as usual after soaking and brushing. To keep the shoes clean, set them on paper and apply several coats of spray starch or fabric protector. They will stay clean longer and soil will wash out more easily.

Cleaning White Leather Athletic Shoes

These can be cleaned easily with whitewall tire cleaner. Take the shoes outside if possible or spray over newspaper. Let sit 2 or 3 minutes and then wipe with paper towels or old rags. Remember, whitewall tire cleaner is a bleaching product, so rinse shoes thoroughly before wearing in the house on carpet. Pay special attention to the soles.

Polishing White Leather

Before polishing, clean well. To remove scuffs, try an art gum eraser or a paste of baking soda and water. To cover scuffs that won't come off, use liquid typewriter correction fluid prior to polishing. Prep the shoes for white polish by rubbing them with the cut side of a raw potato. The potato will help the polish go on smoothly and cover scuff marks.

When You're Out of Shoe Polish

Reach for the furniture polish. Take a rag and spray liberally with furniture polish. Rub the shoe well and buff. In a real hurry, use baby wipes! Rub on and buff.

Fixing Scuffs and Tears on Shoes

If there's a black mark on shoes, try a dab of nail polish remover, rubbing alcohol or lighter fluid on a clean cloth. For areas where the color is removed try using a marker in the same color. Wipe immediately after applying with a paper towel and then polish.

Scuffs on Gold or Silver Shoes

Use an old, dry toothbrush with white toothpaste to remove the scuff; polish with clear polish or furniture polish.

Polishing Patent Leather

Rub petroleum jelly into patent leather and buff with a soft cloth. It not only polishes, it prevents cracking.

Scuff Marks on Vinyl or Plastic Shoes

Use lighter fluid. Be sure to dispose of the rag or paper towel you use outside.

If Plastic Tips Fall Off Your Shoelaces

Easy—twist the ends of the shoelaces and dip in clear nail polish.

To Keep Children's Shoes Tied

Dampen the laces with a spray of water before you tie them. This allows you to tie the bows tighter and the laces will stay in place.

29

Turning Down the Heat on Fire Damage

I honestly hope that you never have any reason to do any thing more than just glance through this chapter, but if you ever have a fire in your home, remember it's here. I spent 15 years as the owner of a disaster restoration company in

Michigan and I can tell you that in those first hours after a fire it's all you can do to remember your name.

The fire truck has just left and there you stand amid what once was your home and is now a smelly, wet, black mess that you hardly recognize. You want to sit down and have a good cry, but there isn't any place clean to sit. What do you do now? Is everything ruined? This chapter will help you deal with the emotional turmoil and give you sound information about what you, as the homeowner, need to do.

Just in Case

First, as soon as you are done reading this, put your home-owner's policy, along with your agent's name and phone number, in a fireproof box or bank safety deposit box. This enables you to easily find them and protects them from being destroyed in the fire. Make notes from this chapter and put them with your insurance information.

Get on the Phone

After the fire is out, call your insurance agent or the 800 number that is often provided on your policy to report claims.

Call immediately. It may seem like the damage couldn't be worse, but it could. After a fire there can be ongoing damage from acid soot residue. Fire produces two main pollutants—nitrous oxide (from burning wood, food, etc.) and sulfur dioxide (from burning plastics and petroleum by-products, etc.). When these pollutants combine with moisture and humidity, they form acid! Within hours this can cause substantial and continuing damage. Prompt attention from your local disaster restoration firm will eliminate the problem and prevent further damage to valuables. Disaster restoration companies are listed in your phone directory and are available 24 hours a day for emergencies. They will preserve, protect and secure surfaces that may be subject to continuing damage, and will work with your insurance adjuster to estimate the damage.

What Is an Insurance Adjuster?

The insurance adjuster works for the insurance company. He is an expert in smoke damage, such as chimney fires, furnace backups and actual fire damage. He will help you decide what can be saved and what can't. He will require a written estimate from a disaster restoration company and any contractors or dry cleaners who will participate in the cleanup. Sometimes more than one estimate will be requested.

During this time you will be receiving all kinds of comments and advice from friends, relatives and even strangers. Ignore it! Your insurance adjuster is a professional and knows the best way to handle smoke damage. The adjuster may even be able to give you advice on a company that they have dealt with before if you are unsure who to call.

Disaster Restoration Companies

Disaster restoration companies (i.e. cleaning companies) do two types of cleaning: structural and contents cleaning. Structural cleaning is wall-washing, carpet cleaning, cupboards—the things you can't remove from the house when you move. Contents cleaning is the upholstery, hard furniture, dishes, clothes, etc.—things you take with you when you move. They will provide a complete estimate to the insurance company and a copy to you.

Once coverage is confirmed and appropriate authorizations are secured, the cleaning and repairs will take place as quickly as possible. This will include dry cleaning, laundry and deodorization, also covered in this chapter.

Payment

After completion of all the cleaning and restoration, the insurance company will generally issue a check in your name and in the name of the firm that did the work. Once the work is satisfactory, you sign over the checks.

Deodorization

Deodorization is one of the most important parts of any smoke damage cleanup. Everything smells—even your clothes.

First, the initial odor must be brought under control immediately to make the house habitable, if you are able to live in it during the restoration.

During any reconstruction, exposed interior wall sections will be deodorized and any singed wood will be sealed to prevent odor. In serious fires, deodorization will take place after cleaning, too.

All clothing will have to be deodorized during laundry and dry cleaning, and in serious cases will be put in an ozone room that opens the oxygen molecules and releases odor.

Ozone machines are also used for deodorizing the home, resulting in a smell much like the air after a thunderstorm.

The best deodorization technique I have ever known is recreating the conditions causing the odor. In the case of smoke damage a deodorant "smoke" is produced, which allows the deodorization process to penetrate in exactly the same manner the smoke odor did.

Additional odor control is done with duct sealing and deodorization.

Additionally, all walls that are washed and painted should be sealed first with a special sealer to eliminate residue "bleed through" from the oily smoke film. Then the walls are painted in the normal manner. This process is one that your disaster restoration firm and adjuster will be familiar with.

With light smoke damage, many times the wall washing is necessary, but not painting. Deodorization is generally always advised.

What If You Don't Have Insurance?

The best advice I can give you is to carry insurance. If you live in an apartment or condominium, buy renter's insurance. If smoke damage occurs, you'll be glad you did.

But, if you don't have insurance, here's some helpful advice:

Go to a janitorial supply store and ask their advice on which cleaning chemicals to use. They can provide you with a professional-quality deodorant to wash clothes, linens and hard surfaces. You will put this deodorant in the water that you clean with or wash clothes with.

Call a disaster restoration firm and try to rent an ozone machine to deodorize the structure and your contents, bearing in mind that prolonged ozone use will yellow plastics.

Buy a soot and dirt removal sponge to clean walls. This is somewhat like a blackboard eraser that removes oily smoke film, so that when you begin to wash the walls the sooty film won't smear.

Rent a carpet cleaning machine with an upholstery attachment to clean carpet and all upholstery that can be cleaned with water.

Wash hard furniture with oil soap and dry, then use furniture polish if you want a brighter shine.

Wash Everything

Wash everything thoroughly—this means walls, cupboards, collectibles, dishes, clothes, etc., otherwise the odor will remain.

Start in one room and do it completely except for carpet cleaning (you'll track during the cleaning process and spread soot on the carpet). Clean the carpet in all rooms last.

If you still have odor, do a final deodorization with an ozone machine, or if you can, hire a firm to come in and do it for you.

30

The Big Drip—
Water Damage
Restoration

What a shock! When you left the house everything was fine.

You come home and unlock the door; you walk in and hear the sound of running water. As you step in, water comes up to your ankles. Now you find water running across the carpet and floors and lapping at the legs of furniture as the sofa and chairs try to soak it up. Here's what you need to do immediately.

Turn It Off

First, know where your water shut-off is and use it. Turn off the water and look for the source of the leak. BE SURE THE ELECTRICAL POWER SOURCE IS OFF BEFORE YOU WALK IN STANDING WATER. The leak could be from a toilet, the washing machine hoses, or a broken pipe.

How quickly you react will have impact on what can be saved in your home.

Call the Professionals

Now that you have shut off the water and located the problem, call your insurance agent. Your agent will act quickly to help you, because by the time an adjuster receives the information it is often too late to reverse some of the damage that has taken place.

Wet carpet and pad are restorable if it is taken care of as soon as possible after the damage has occurred.

A professional company that deals in water damage of all kinds can stop further damage from occurring and also save the carpet and pad.

To find a water damage expert, look in the yellow pages under "water damage" or under "cleaning companies" or "disaster restoration firms." Be sure to get a company that specializes in this problem.

Dry Out

First they will extract water from the pad and the carpet and treat both with an EPA-registered disinfectant. They will then install drying equipment, which consists of high-powered carpet blowers that are slipped between the carpet and the pad. They also will install dehumidification equipment to facilitate drying. They will advise you to keep your home's interior temperature at 70 degrees or warmer for ideal drying conditions. This drying equipment will also facilitate drying of upholstered furniture and walls as it dries the carpet.

Upholstered furniture will need to have water extracted from it and be treated with an EPA-registered disinfectant, too. Wood furniture will be wiped down and allowed to dry.

The water damage restoration firm will check, usually every 24 hours, to see how the drying process is coming and to move equipment to continue the drying process.

What Is an Antimicrobial?

Many water damage restoration firms have a wonderful antimicrobial product available that not only disinfects, but also inhibits the growth of mold, mildew and bacterial

spores. This is applied to the carpet after extraction takes place and has certainly saved many a carpet.

After all the carpet and contents of your home are dry, the upholstery and carpet will be cleaned and again treated with a disinfectant product or antimicrobial. Hard furniture will be washed and polished and hard floors will be given a final cleaning. If your carpet or upholstery had a protective coating on it, this will be reapplied.

Walls will be washed as needed and your home will be returned to normal once again.

Answers to Your Sea of Worries

The Pad Will Dissolve!

Not so! Most pads are made of nonwater-sensitive foam bonded with a dry solvent-soluble adhesive.

The Seams Will Separate!

Now that is logical. Wet carpet naturally means shrinkage, right? WRONG! Nonwater-soluble adhesives are used on seams. Regardless of what happens, seams can be repaired.

The Carpet Shrank Off the Wall!

Only poorly installed carpet will come loose from the wall and this is easily restretched.

The Carpet Will Fall Apart!

This is not likely. During the manufacturing process carpet manufacturers actually immerse carpet in water many times during the dyeing and rinsing process. Synthetic fibers, the primary backings, and latex adhesives are virtually unaffected by water for at least 48 hours.

Sewer Backups

If your water damage is due to a sewer backup, these restoration firms are trained to deal with it. Stay out of the water and waste. Let the trained experts deal with the water and bacterial problems; that's their job and they know what can be saved and what can't.

31

Taking the Atchoo-Cough-Cough Out of Your Air Ducts

Picture yourself in this situation: You have had smoke damage in your home. All the cleaning and repainting is done and now you are ready to turn on the furnace. You go to the thermostat and turn it up. You hear the furnace spring to life. The central blower is activated . . . and, suddenly, you run screaming from the house. What's wrong? All the odor that collected in the duct system during the smoke damage has just been blown full force from the duct system and into the house. It smells like the house is on fire again. As if the smell isn't enough, you now see black soot residue blowing out in a dark cloud and settling all over the newly cleaned walls, carpet and furniture. How could this happen? Nobody thought to clean the duct system prior to cleaning the house and turning on the furnace.

Duct cleaning and deodorizing is not just for houses that have had fire or smoke damage. It is very beneficial in older homes where dust and allergy-causing bacteria have accumulated in the duct work and are blown through the home each time the furnace runs. Duct cleaning can be very beneficial for people who have allergy problems, too.

What Is Duct Cleaning?

Duct cleaning consists of removing register covers and vacuuming out all the duct work that leads to the furnace. After some elaborate preparatory vacuuming and cleaning procedures, which include cleaning all the register covers, a duct sealer is introduced into the system in the form of a fine mist. This sealer is a plastic-like resin. The chemical itself actually neutralizes odor and seals onto the interior walls of the system the loose soot, dust and dirt that remain after vacuuming. During this process all odor is eliminated and minor residues remaining in unseen or unreachable areas are permanently sealed onto the interior surface of the ducts.

This process gives you a dirt-, dust- and pollen-free environment. If allergies run in your family you will immediately notice the difference. This is particularly good in older homes that, naturally, have the original duct systems in place.

When you have this procedure done it is a good idea to have your furnace cleaned at the same time. Many furnace companies clean duct work, too, as do many disaster restoration or cleaning companies.

Fresh Air

You've had smoke damage . . . you have allergies . . . you just purchased an older home. . . . This is some healthy advice for cleaner air and a fresher smell.

32
Stop the Science Experiment— Mold and Mildew

Left unchecked, dampness in a home or basement can rot wood, peel paint and promote rust and mildew.

Find the Source

Here is a simple test to determine if dampness is caused by seepage or excessive humidity:

Cut several 12-inch squares of aluminum foil. Tape them

in various spots on the floor and walls; seal the edges tightly. If moisture collects between the foil and the surface after several days, waterproof the interior walls. If moisture forms on the foil's surface, take the following steps:

Close windows on humid days.

Install a window exhaust fan.

Vent your clothes dryer to the outside.

Use a dehumidifier, especially during summer months.

Treat walls with epoxy-based waterproofing paint or masonry sealer. (To clean walls in preparation for paint, look for special mildew cleaners in home centers.)

Make Your Own Treatment

You can also make your own mildew treatment by mixing a quart of chlorine bleach and a tablespoon of powdered non-ammoniated laundry detergent with 3 quarts of warm water. Scrub the mildew-stained surface with the solution and allow it to work until the discoloration vanishes, rinse thoroughly and allow to dry.

Caution

Be sure to wear goggles, rubber gloves and protective clothing when using this solution. Never allow it to come in contact with carpet or fabrics, and clean the shoes you wear before walking on carpets. Do this in a well-ventilated area.

Resource Guide

ACT NATURAL CLOTHS™: See Euronet USA.

ART GUM ERASER: You remember the little brownish-tan rectangular eraser that you used in school, the one that crumbled as you erased? That's the one!

BAKING POWDER: If you bake, you already have this in the cupboard. If not, look in the baking section near the baking soda. Baking powder and baking soda are not the same thing, so don't even go there!

BEESWAX: Is usually found in drugstores, hardware stores and natural product stores. If you don't see it, ask!

BITTER APPLE: This keeps pets from dining on your plants, etc. It is not harmful to them, but tastes terrible so it discourages them entirely. Look for it at pet supply stores.

BORAX: Better known as Twenty Mule Team Borax, this laundry additive can be found in the detergent aisle.

BRUCE FLOOR CARE PRODUCTS: Look for these

products at hardware stores, home centers and wherever wood flooring is sold.

CALGON WATER SOFTENER®: Look for it with the laundry additives at the grocery store.

CHAMOIS: Found in hardware stores and home centers.

CHARCOAL: This is the type made for fish tanks and is available at pet supply stores.

CLEAR AMMONIA: There are two types of ammonia, clear and sudsy. Clear contains no soap and should be used where suggested for that reason.

COLD CREAM: Plain old Ponds that your grandma used on her face, or the store brand.

CUTICLE REMOVER: The gel you apply to your cuticles to soften them. Let's be clear, it is cuticle remover, NOT nail polish remover.

DENATURED ALCOHOL: This is an industrial alcohol reserved for heavy-duty cleaning. Don't use it near open flame and dispose of any rags that were used to apply it outside the home. Launder or clean anything that you treat with it as soon as possible. Look for this in cans at hardware stores and home centers. Remember the Queen's rule: always test in an inconspicuous place before treating a large area with this product.

ENERGINE CLEANING FLUID®: Look for this at the hardware store, the home center and even in some grocery stores (usually on the top shelf with the laundry additives).

EURONET USA: Makers of the Act Natural™ microfiber cloths and mops. They clean and disinfect without chemicals using only water. They have been scientifically proven to kill germs and bacteria and even come with a warranty. They are easy to use, great for people with allergies, and can be cleaned and sanitized in the washer (this is particularly important with the mop). Use them in the kitchen, bathroom, to spot carpet, on windows, mirrors, hard furniture, in the car, virtually anywhere you clean. Call 888-638-2882 or visit www.euronetusa.com. They are a wonderful investment. My mop is almost two years old and is still doing the job.

FELS-NAPTHA SOAP®: What a wonderful laundry spotter and cleaner this is. You'll find it in the bar soap section of the grocery store. It's usually on the bottom shelf in a small stack and always has dust on it, because nobody knows what to use it for.

FINE DRYWALL SANDPAPER: This sandpaper looks like window screen. Make sure you buy a package marked "fine grade."

FINE STEEL WOOL: Look for the symbol "0000" and the word FINE. And don't try soap-filled steel wool pads. They are not acceptable substitutes.

GLYCERIN: Look for glycerin in drugstores in the hand cream section. Always purchase plain glycerin, not the type containing rosewater.

GO-JO WATERLESS HAND CLEANER®: People with greasy hands have used this product for years. It's a hand cleaner and so much more. Look for it at home centers and hardware stores.

HYDROGEN PEROXIDE: Choose the type that you use on cuts and to gargle with—not the type used to bleach hair. That will remove color from carpet or fabric.

INVISIBLE SHIELD® SURFACE TREATMENT: This is such a wonderful product that just the name gives me goose bumps! It turns all of those hard to clean surfaces in your home (tub, shower, shower doors, sinks, counters, stovetops, windows, any surface that is not wood or painted) into non-stick surfaces that can be cleaned with water and a soft cloth. No more soap scum or hard-water deposits! It never builds up on surfaces so it won't make them slippery, and it's non-toxic, so you can use it on dishes and food surfaces too. Call 800-528-3149 to find a supplier near you.

LEMON OR ORANGE EXTRACT: These are found in the spice area of the grocery store where vanilla extract is sold.

LINSEED OIL: You'll find this at the hardware store, usually in the paint and staining section. It is combustible, so use care in disposing of rags or paper towels used to apply it. Keep it in the garage or basement away from open flame.

MEAT TENDERIZER: Use the unseasoned variety please, or you will have a whole new stain to deal with. Store brands work fine.

NAIL POLISH REMOVER: I caution you to use nonacetone polish remover, which is much less aggressive than acetone polish remover. (Straight acetone is exceedingly strong.) Use only where recommended and with great care. Look for this product at beauty supply stores.

NATURAL SPONGE: A natural sponge is the best sponge you will ever use. It has hundreds of natural "scrubbing fingers" that make any wall-washing job speed by. Look for these at home centers and hardware stores and choose a nice size to fit your hand. Wash them in lukewarm water with gentle suds. You can put them in the washing machine if you avoid combining them with fabrics that have lint.

NATURE'S MIRACLE®: An enzyme-based odor removal product for urine-based pet accidents. Available at pet supply stores across the country.

NON-GEL TOOTHPASTE: This is just a fancy name for old-fashioned plain white toothpaste. Gels just don't work, so don't even try.

ODORZOUT®: A fabulous, dry, 100 percent natural deodorizer. It's nontoxic, so you can use it any place you have a smell or a stink. It is especially effective on pet urine odors, and since it is used dry it is simple to apply. Call 800-88STINK, or visit their website at www.88stink.com.

OIL OF CLOVES: Widely available at health food stores, vitamin stores and natural food stores.

OUTRIGHT PET ODOR ELIMINATOR®: An enzyme odor removal product for urine-based pet accidents. Available at pet supply stores across the country.

POWDERED ALUM: This old-fashioned product was once used in pickling. Look for it at drugstores and if you can't find it, ask the pharmacist.

ROTTENSTONE: Mild pumice, look for it at hardware stores and home centers.

RUST REMOVER: These are serious products so follow the directions carefully. Look for products like Whink® and Rust Magic® at hardware stores and home centers.

SADDLE SOAP: You will find this in the hardware store, or in the shoe polish section at most any store.

SHAVING CREAM: The cheaper brands work fine and shaving cream works better than gel.

SOAPWORKS: Manufacturer of wonderful nontoxic, user- and earth-friendly cleaning, laundry and personal care products. Try their At Home All-Purpose Cleaner™, originally designed for allergy and asthma sufferers. Soapworks products are very effective, and they are economical, so everyone can use them. Call 800-699-9917 or visit their website at www.soapworks.com.

SOOT AND DIRT REMOVAL SPONGE: These are used to clean walls, wallpaper, lampshades and even soot. They also remove pet hair from upholstery. These big brick erasers are available at home centers and hardware stores, usually near the wallpaper supplies. Clean them by washing in a pail of warm water and liquid dish soap, rinse well and allow to dry before using again.

SPOT SHOT INSTANT CARPET STAIN REMOVER®: My all-time favorite carpet spotter and I have tried them all! Try SPOT SHOT UPHOLSTERY STAIN REMOVER® too. Available most everywhere, or call 800-848-4389.

SQUEEGEE: When buying a squeegee for washing windows, look for a good quality one with a replaceable rubber blade. Always be sure that the rubber blade is soft and flexible for best results. Look for these at hardware stores, home centers and janitorial supply companies. They come in different widths, so be sure to think about the size windows, etc., that you are going to use it for. A 12-inch blade is a good starting point.

TACK-TRAP®: Bugs are drawn to the color of this sticky sheet. Sold in garden supply stores and some hardware stores.

TANG™ BREAKFAST DRINK: Yes, this is the product that the astronauts took to the moon! It is also a great cleaner. (Store brands work just as well.)

TRISODIUM PHOSPHATE (TSP): Cleaning professionals have used this product for years. It is wonderful for washing walls, garage floors and any tough cleaning job. Look for it at hardware stores, home centers and janitorial supply stores. Wear rubber gloves when using it.

TYPEWRITER ERASER: A thing of the past, but still available at office supply stores. Shaped like a pencil with a little brush where the pencil eraser would be, they can be sharpened like a pencil and will last for years.

WASHING SODA: I like Arm & Hammer™ Washing Soda, which can be found in the detergent aisle at the grocery store along with other laundry additives. No, you can not substitute baking soda, it is a different product!

WAX CRAYONS: These are sold in hardware stores and home centers and come in various wood colors for concealing scratches in wood surfaces. Don't be fooled by the color name; try to take along a sample of what you need to patch to get the best possible match.

WD-40™ LUBRICANT: I bet you will find a can in your garage or basement. Fine spray oil for lubricating all kinds of things, it's a wonderful product for regenerating grease so that it can be removed from clothes. Look for WD-40™ at the hardware store, home center and even the grocery store.

WHITING: Look for this at the hardware store, usually near the paint.

WINDOW SCRUBBER: This looks like a squeegee wearing a coat. Look for it at janitorial supply stores and home centers.

WINE AWAY RED WINE STAIN REMOVER™: This unbelievable product can remove red stains, such as red wine, red pop, cranberry juice, red food coloring, grape juice, etc., from carpet and fabric. It is totally nontoxic and made from fruit and vegetable extracts. I just can't believe how well it works! Look for it where liquor is sold or call 888-WINE-AWAY for a store location near you.

WINTERGREEN OIL: Widely available at health food stores, natural food stores and some linen stores.

ZUD HEAVY DUTY CLEANSER®: This is a wonderful cleanser for really tough jobs. It works great on rust on hard surfaces too. Find it at hardware stores, home centers and grocery stores. Well worth keeping on hand.

Index

acrylic paintings, 97
acrylic spray, 129
Act Natural Mop™, 38
air ducts, 149–51
air freshener, 25, 87
allergies, 22, 24, 150, 151
alum, 3
aluminum, 108
aluminum foil: for bathtub
  decals, 5; for chrome, 20, 118;
  for grill, 104; under ironing
  board cover, 90; for rust on
  chrome, 32, 118; for silver
  cutlery, 17–18; to test for
  humidity, 152–53
ammonia: for air freshener, 87;
  for broiler pans, 8; for burner
  rings and guards, 10; for carpets, 73; for ceramic tile, 36;
  for chrome, 10; for cooktops,
  15; for gold, 20; for grills,
  104–05; for marble, 58, 59;
  for ovens, 14; for screens,
  124; for silver-cleaning cloths,
  18; for stainless steel, 17; for

walls, 45; for windows, 123
answering machines, 93
antimicrobial product, 146–47
antistatic product, 92, 94
ants, 132–33
aphids, 131–32
appliances, kitchen, 7–8, 81
artificial flowers, 129
asthma, 22
At Home All-Purpose Cleaner™,
  22

babies, 77–83
baby oil, 19, 42
baby wipes, 136
bacteria, 146–47, 148, 150
baking powder, 58, 135
baking soda, 24; for air freshener, 25, 87; for battery cor-
  rosion, 118; for bugs, 27, 123;
  for burned-on food, 27; for
  car odors, 86; for carpets, 66;
  for clothes, 26–27; for compact discs, 93; for cooktops,
  15; for countertops, 28; for

Your Personal Tips and Hints

Your Personal Tips and Hints

NOW YOU CAN TALK DIRTY WITH

The Queen of Clean®

EVERY OTHER MONTH!

If you enjoyed the book, you're sure to enjoy a subscription to QUEEN OF CLEAN®—The Newsletter for just $19.50 per year. You'll receive 6 issues, one every other month. Each 8-page issue is loaded with cleaning information, tips and answers to subscriber questions. Just send your order to the address below and the Queen will start your subscription immediately!

Now Available—Other Queen of Clean Products!

Plus, you can order these products tested and approved by the Queen herself. Each one designed to make cleaning chores a little less, well, dirty.

TELESCOPING LAMBSWOOL DUSTER (Item #101)

Washable dusters will last up to 10 years depending on care and usage. Use on fans, lights, furniture, blinds, ceilings, baseboards, everything! Only $12 each plus $3.95 shipping and handling.

LAMBSWOOL DUST MITT (Item #102)

Never use dusting chemicals again with this over-the-hand duster. See the beauty that the lanolin in the duster can bring to your hard surfaces. Lasts up to 10 years and easily washes clean. A must to simplify all your dusting chores. Only $10 each plus $3 shipping and handling.

PALACE POTTY PUFF (Item #103)

The answer to your toilet cleaning problems! It lasts for years and won't scratch or rust. Can be disinfected with a little chlorine bleach in your toilet bowl. Self-wringing so your hands never touch the water. Only $4.50 each plus $3 shipping and handling.

QUEEN OF CLEAN® APRON (Item #104)

Royal blue twill-type fabric with full pockets across the front, ties at neck and waist for custom fit. Across the front, in yellow letters with red shadowing it says, "TALK DIRTY TO ME." Beneath that, in smaller letters, it declares, "I Know the Queen of Clean!" Perfect for a woman, or as a barbecue apron for a man. Only $12 each plus $3 shipping and handling.

Check or credit card orders only, please! Be sure to provide your name, address and telephone number so we can contact you in the event of any questions about your order.

If ordering by credit card, please include card type (VISA, Master Card), account number, expiration date and your signature along with the item number(s) and the required shipping and handling charges plus applicable sales tax to:

QUEEN OF CLEAN
PO BOX 655
PEORIA, AZ 85380

Or order at **www.queenofclean.com**   Thank you for your order!

COMING SOON IN PAPERBACK

Talking Dirty Laundry
with the
Queen of Clean®
Linda Cobb

Now that she's helped you hone your housekeeping talents, wait 'til you see what her Royal Highness can do for your clothes! With hundreds of fast, fun, and ingenious tips for the "laundry challenged," the Queen of Clean offers freedom from the shackles of the spin-cycle and takes the stress out of washing, ironing, and stain-busting forever!

Also available as an e-book

Pocket Books
A VIACOM COMPANY
www.SimonSays.com

Visit www.QueenofClean.com

Queen of Clean® is a registered trademark of Linda Cobb and is the property of Queen and King Enterprises, Inc.

3063